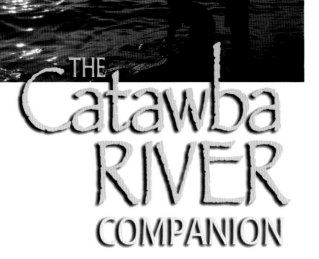

THE
Catawba
RIVER
COMPANION

Sponsored by Duke Power

Duke Power.

A Duke Energy Company

Palmetto Conservation Foundation/PCF Press
With photography by Bill Price
© 2003

PCF *Press*

Published by Palmetto Conservation Foundation/PCF Press
PO Box 1984
Spartanburg, SC 29304
© 2003 Palmetto Conservation Foundation

First edition, 2003
10 9 8 7 6 5 4 3 2 1

Manufactured in Hong Kong.

Text: Diane Milks, Yon Lambert, Louise Pettus
Maps, design, layout & production: Sandy Husmann/
Palmetto Conservation Foundation.
Proofreading: Victoria Reed/Readable Ink.
Photographer: Unless otherwise noted, Bill Price.
Review and project support: John Garton, Jennifer Huff,
Robert Siler, Lindsay Pettus.

On the cover: The wildlife overlook at Cowans Ford
Wildlife Refuge on the Catawba River. Photo courtesy
Mecklenburg County. Additional photos (top to bottom):
Landsford Canal State Park ranger Don Oneppo
paddling on the Catawba. The "headwaters" of the
Catawba River: Catawba Falls near Old Fort, NC. The rare
Rocky Shoals Spider lily in full bloom on the Catawba
River. An aerial view of the Catawba River.

Library of Congress Cataloging-in-Publication Data

Milks, Diane, 1962-
  The Catawba River companion / Diane Milks, Yon Lambert ;
with photography by Bill Price.
     p. cm.
Includes bibliographical references (p.) and index.
  ISBN 0-9679016-8-5 (pbk.)
  1. Catawba River Valley (N.C. and S.C.)--Guidebooks. 2. Lakes--
North Carolina--Guidebooks. 3. Lakes--South Carolina--
Guidebooks. 4. Catawba River Valley (N.C. and S.C.)--Pictorial
works. I. Lambert, Yon, 1971-II. Title.
  F262.C3 M55 2003
  917.57'450444--dc21

                        2002015371

Lake James
Mt. Mitchell
Old Fort • Marion
Ridgecrest •
Asheville •
Morganton • Hickory
Lake Hickory
Mooresville •
Lake Norman
Huntersville •
Mountain Island Lake
Gastonia •
Charlotte •
South Fork River
Lake Wylie
Fort Mill •
Rock Hill •
Broad River
Saluda River
Greenville •
Great Falls
Lancaster •
Catawba River
Lake Greenwood
Lake Wateree
Columbia •
Wateree River
Lake Murray
Congaree River
Rimini •
Santee River
Georgetor
Lake Marion
Lake Moultrie
Monck's Corner •
Cooper River
Charleston •

Table of Contents

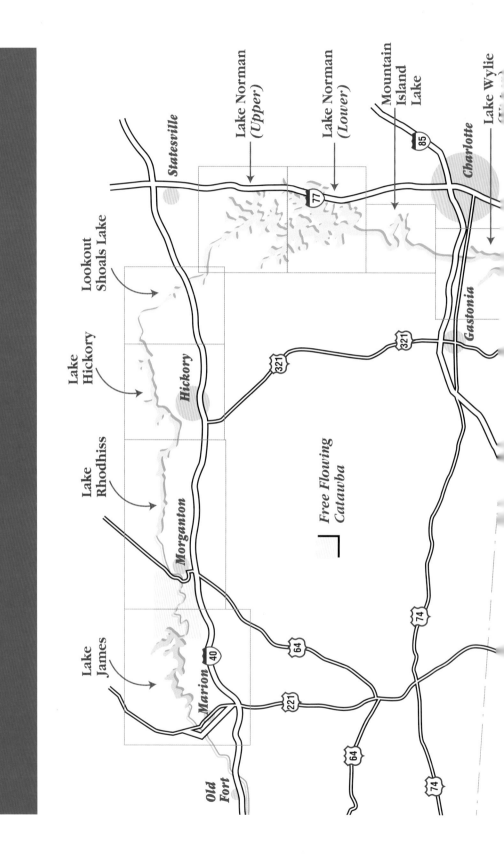

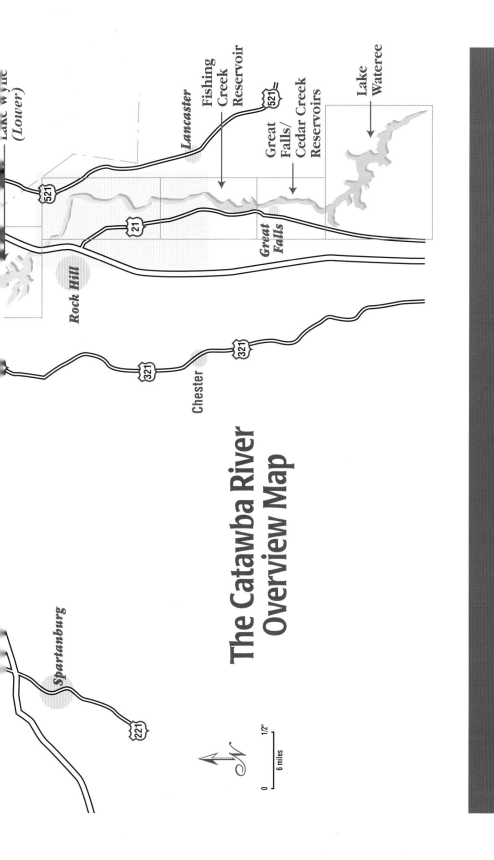

The Catawba River
Overview Map

Lake Wylie (Lower)

Lancaster

Fishing Creek Reservoir

Great Falls/ Cedar Creek Reservoirs

Lake Wateree

521

521

521

21

321

321

221

Rock Hill

Chester

Great Falls

Spartanburg

N

0   1/2"
6 miles

The Catawba River Companion

Ten miles below Mount Mitchell, the tallest peak east of the Mississippi River, the Catawba River springs to life. It flows from that humble beginning to become a mighty force, flowing for most of its 225 miles through the most populated areas of North Carolina and South Carolina. More than 1.5 million people depend on the river and its 11 reservoirs for electricity, drinking water, wastewater discharge industrial uses and recreation.

The Catawba River is the birthplace of Duke Power, or Southern Power, as the Company was called at the time of its beginnings in 1904. Today, the river supports half of Duke Power's generation and is home to acres of forests and lively ecosystems.

For nearly 100 years, Duke Power has been privileged to be a partner in the stewardship of natural resources such as those you'll see on your trip down the river. Whether it's bird-watching at the Mountain Island Lake Educational State Forest or enjoying the beautiful Rocky Shoals Spider Lily at Landsford Canal – the Catawba River holds opportunities for all.

PHOTO COURTESY OF MECKLENBURG COUNTY.

Duke scientist John Garton demonstrating his infectious love for all things wild on the Catawba. John retired in 2002.

Our thanks to the Palmetto Conservation Foundation and others who developed this companion guide for the Catawba River. They have truly captured the heart and beauty of one of our region's greatest assets.

Bill Coley

President, Duke Power

Grandfather Mountain is also a part of the Catawba watershed.

Introduction

I t is a drizzly, gray March morning on the Catawba River in Burke County, North Carolina. From the edge of a pier overlooking Lake Rhodhiss, we can trace two baited fishing lines down into the murky water. And while the lake usually offers trophy-sized largemouths and walleye, this rig will be lucky to lure a bluegill. Local fishermen like to thank 1989's Hurricane Hugo for blessing Rhodhiss with the most lay-down trees of any lake its size in North Carolina. Behind us, the parking area at the Rhodhiss Access Area is deserted. The steep, 47-step staircase creased into a hill separating the two-tiered lot leads up into gray mist. It is discernibly lonely.

Normally we would prefer a more idyllic beginning for our trip down the Catawba River; say the clatter of the river's commonly accepted headwaters at Catawba Falls or perhaps the Linville River tucked many miles away amid the weathered peaks and passes of Linville Gorge. Instead, we're here, overlooking one of the smaller lakes in this river system and dangling our feet in the cold water. This will do. For all practical purposes, this is as good a place as any to begin exploring the Catawba River corridor.

We like this spot because, at first glance, the Catawba is no longer a wild and dramatic river. Rather — and like many places in the Carolinas — it has a familiar, domestic feel. If we were to float it from Lake James, NC to Lake Wateree, SC, we would travel more than 225 miles through dashes of whitewater, around 11 dams, across placid lakes and shoals. We could ogle its many species of fish, birds and floral displays. We might stop off to visit the world's largest colony of the rare Rocky Shoals Spider lily or a renowned raptor center, camp on a remote island or enjoy a dinner cruise on Lake Norman. And yet, to most residents of the Carolinas, a trip of this sort would seem as preposterous as a bicycle tour along Interstate 40.

Although the Catawba River is the

Fire Pink

major physical connection between the mountains to the Piedmont, it is celebrated today more for its utilitarian value than its natural features. Over the course of the last century, as we have farmed its banks and used its current to remove waste, the Catawba slowly morphed from a free-flowing waterway into a liquid locomotive so completely a part of our environment that we sometimes fail to stop and consider it a "river" at all.

PHOTO COURTESY OF MECKLENBURG COUNTY

Cowans Ford Wildlife Refuge in winter.

That's a shame.

That's also where *The Catawba River Companion* comes in.

The objective of this guide is to include a cross section of information about what visitors can see and do along the Catawba River corridor. We have included maps and additional resources showing places to hike, camp, fish, swim, dine, paddle, mountain bike and ride horses. Along the way, we hope you'll learn something about the region's natural history and take the time to explore the valley's flora and fauna. With this guide in tow, you'll be able to enjoy many years of exploration on and around the Catawba River.

More importantly, we hope you'll come away with a better appreciation for the river's place in our natural world, even on a dreary winter's morning at a deserted fishing pier. A few river miles east of Lake Rhodhiss, the waters of the Catawba lap quietly onto the banks at River Bend Park. From the water, towering hardwoods camouflage the 450-acre forest and one might never guess it holds more than a dozen miles of trails, picnic areas and grassy meadows teeming with wildlife. Like the Catawba itself, one needs merely to get off the beaten path to open a treasure trove of opportunity. So come with us as we explore the Catawba River from mountains to Piedmont. You may well be surprised at what you discover…

How To Use This Book

A fter the Introduction, *The Catawba River Companion* includes one section for each lake. Each lake includes notes about riverside recreation, lakeside camping and nearby "bed & breakfasts" plus more in-depth text for enjoyable day trips and bigger "destination" sites in the area.

Day Trips are local places where visitors could while away a few hours at the foot of a waterfall, mountain biking a wooded trail, or learning about history and culture. An icon signifies Day Trips and looks like this:

Destinations are the key attractions near each lake. These are usually popular sites such as wilderness areas and parks but they might also include visitor centers or botanical gardens. An icon signifies "Destinations" and looks like this:

A map keyed to each lake opens each section while an overview map in the Introduction helps tie everything together. The book also includes an appendix packed with helpful resources.

If you are interested in exploring the Catawba, it might be smart to begin with the Introduction where you can get a feel for the river's history and natural environment. Then see if some interesting place catches your eye on the overview. Didn't realize there were so many hiking destinations around Mountain Island Lake? Just flip to that section for more details. Take some time to browse through *The Catawba River Companion* and find the hidden gems along this river corridor, home to dozens of parks, natural areas and wilderness settings.

Copperhead Island

The River's Course

For the purposes of this book, the Catawba River runs from the Blue Ridge Mountains near Mount Mitchell and flows 225 miles through the Carolina Piedmont to Lake Wateree near Columbia. In truth, the river runs further – another 200 or more miles into the Atlantic as the Wateree and Santee rivers. Like the Yadkin-Pee Dee River to the east, the Catawba-Wateree-Santee system is essentially one river known by three names for both practical and political reasons. Many would argue that any discussion of the Catawba should also include the Wateree and Santee. We recognize those concerns but choose to focus on the upper reaches of the system, essentially from Lake James to Lake Wateree.

In the Old Fort, NC area, locals like to say the Catawba really begins with three small streams in McDowell County each producing "a trickle that is taxed to fill the hand."[1] Even once they converge, the stream is barely six feet wide and its clean waters taste earthy and rich. From here the Catawba flows freely north and east for around 20 miles – dropping nearly 1,000 feet over numerous waterfalls along the way – until it opens into a wide, silty swath near a junction with the Catawba North Fork. At first glance it's tempting to call this point the Catawba's first metamorphosis into a series of lakes. That would be unjust. In truth, the river and Lake James are worlds apart. On the west side, the proletarian Catawba has already passed Marion, NC and its banks are peppered with waterfront homes, access areas and a state park. On the east, the lake created by the natural and scenic Linville River is remote and standoffish, surrounded by undeveloped, wild land. When water levels rose after being impounded by an elaborate dam system, the overflow spilled through a canal and formed what most of us call Lake James. Today the riverbed immediately downstream of the Catawba River dam is a series of beaver ponds and extensive wetlands, fed by a few small tributaries.

The main stem of the river now flows through Duke Power's Bridgewater Hydro Station at Linville Dam, heading almost due east to the manufacturing towns of Morganton and Valdese. These are places that have been shaped by and adapted to reflect the river itself, with roots in textiles, furniture and forestry. Here one would barely consider

> ...the Catawba really begins with three small streams in McDowell County each producing "a trickle that is taxed to fill the hand."

this a river at all; more accurately it is two narrow lakes — Rhodhiss and Hickory — featuring many private piers, public boat ramps and several waterside parks.

At a bend just east of Lake Hickory, the Catawba cuts hard to the south and becomes Lookout Shoals Lake. To a geologist, the metamorphic ridge of rock that created the shoals offers one of the most dramatic points on the river. Were it not for the eons-old obstacle created by this ridge, the Catawba might have wandered lazily east instead of making a beeline south into South Carolina and setting a course for human population in our region. Lookout Shoals is also not far from where the Catawba morphs into the "inland sea" better known as Lake Norman. With more than 590 miles of shoreline and almost 32,000 acres of surface area, the Catawba here is only a river by the wildest stretch of the imagination. At one point, with the lake more than a mile wide, winds whip the open waters into whitecaps reminiscent of the ocean. The lake is home to more than 90 marinas, access areas, a state park and tens of thousands of piers and slips. It is not an undiscovered resource.

Still, the current persists, flowing south through the Cowans Ford Hydro Station and into Mountain Island Lake, home to nature preserves, forests, wildlife refuges and historic sites. Though not well known outside the region, this lake is hugely popular with visitors who enjoy amenities such as the Carolina Raptor Center,

(continued to page 16)

The 30-mile stretch of the Catawba River flowing from Lake Wylie to Fishing Creek Reservoir is among the prettiest on the entire river.

How Did The River Get Its Name?

No one is sure how the Catawba River got its name. As late as 1894, Judge Matthew Locke McCorkle touted one folk tradition that "Catawba" was Indian for "catfish," since so many of the fish were found in its waters. Others have connected the river and the grape of the same name.

Early 20th century anthropologists claimed the word "Catawba" is rooted in the Choctaw sound "kat a pa." Related to the language of numerous Southeastern Indian groups, it is loosely translated as "to divide or separate, to break."

— *Catawba County Historical Association*

Different varieties of freshwater catfish.

(continued from page 15)

county-maintained horse trails and historic sites in the Latta Plantation Nature Preserve. To naturalists, this is one of the richest areas of the Carolinas although you need a boat to see some of the last (and best) undeveloped areas. In coming years, the North Carolina Division of Forest Resources will open interpretive facilities at Mountain Island Educational State Forest. After Mountain Island Lake, the Catawba continues under Interstate 85, past a junction with its own South Fork and into South Carolina.

Here the river becomes the many-fingered Lake Wylie — the oldest of Duke's "power" lakes — before reverting yet again into its former self for the second of two significant free-flowing sections. This 30-mile stretch, which flows past Landsford Canal State Park to Fishing Creek Reservoir, is among the prettiest on the entire river. Downstream of Fishing Creek, the river forms Great Falls and Cedar Creek reservoirs, followed by Lake Wateree. For our purposes, the Catawba ends as it flows into Lake Wateree, an impoundment created in 1919. Here, the river becomes known as the Wateree River and flows approximately 70 miles to its confluence with the Congaree River. After this confluence, the river flows to the Atlantic Ocean under the name Santee River. When it enters the Atlantic, water that bubbled from a modest spring in McDowell County has traveled more than 400 miles.

Catawba River History

The Catawba River valley has been home to humans for thousands of years. Although our humid climate has all but obliterated most traces of their passing, some of the older artifacts found by archaeologists date to *c.* 8000 B.C. Still, save pieces of pottery and the records of Spanish explorers who traveled among the Indians, little vestiges remain from before European settlement. At that time, approximately 25,000 Native Americans of various tribes lived in both Carolinas. One of the early legends suggests that all land between the Catawba and Broad rivers was designated a shared hunting ground of the Cherokee and Catawba tribes where permanent settlement was forbidden to prevent border conflicts.[2] Regardless, attracted by the rich, alluvial soils along the riverbanks, Native Americans certainly farmed significant stretches of Catawba. Their name for themselves in their own language is *Yap Ye Iswa* (pronounced yap-yay-iswong), which translates loosely to "people of the river." The associated river lands also provided the clay that allowed them to become master potters and – perhaps more than any other remnant of the Catawba Tribe – demonstrated the people's strong attachment to their land. In early trading days, Native American tribes up and down the Eastern seaboard sought after this intricate and durable pottery.

In 1763, the English gave the Catawbas 144,000 acres near what is today Fort Mill and Rock Hill, SC as a reward for helping the English defeat the French in the French and Indian War.

Despite their obvious attachment to the river, the Catawba Tribe did not settle up its farthest reaches. The people lived on lands around Lookout Shoals as late as the 1600s, but by the 1700s had left their farms for hunting and gathering.[3] When the first white settlers arrived around 1750, the Catawbas had already migrated south where they found milder hills and bottomland for their crops. The Catawbas thrived up until around 1760 when smallpox and other European diseases decimated the tribe, reducing its number to around 1,000.[4]

The Catawbas were well known for their relatively diplomatic association with the European settlers. Before the American Revolution, settlers called the Catawba chiefs "king," as in King Haigler who is widely recognized as the greatest Catawba leader of the colonial period.[5]

(continued to page 19)

What Was The 'King's Bottom'?

Before the American Revolution, settlers called the Catawba chiefs "King," as in King Haigler, recognized as the greatest Catawba leader of the colonial period. In 1763, Haigler — who was later killed in a Shawnee ambush — negotiated the treaties that resulted in the British guaranteeing the Catawbas the area that was to become known as the Catawba Indian Land.

There remains some confusion as to exact locations of Catawba towns but there is proof that the towns were numerous and their locations probably shifted over time.

According to local records, the Indian Land was an area 15 miles square, or 144,000 acres, located on both sides of the Catawba River in present-day York and Lancaster County, SC Land west of the river was largely a prairie, teeming with game and carefully maintained as a vast hunting ground. The tribe's villages were, perhaps with one exception, all on the east side of the Catawba.

The principal Catawba town is thought to have been located on the top of a hill on the south bank of Sugar Creek where it enters the river in Lancaster County. The white leaseholders called it Sugar Town. At, or close by, the same location was "Turkeyhead," which may be a translation by whites of the Indian name. In short, Sugar Town and Turkeyhead may have been the same.

The river bottomland between Twelve Mile Creek and Sugar Creek was so rich that it has long been known as the most fertile of all Catawba River land. The fertility comes from the seasonal flooding that for centuries dumped layer upon layer of topsoil on the bottomland. An early visitor described one vast field of corn and beans that stretched from Twelve Mile Creek to Sugar Creek.

This land was called, then and now, the King's Bottom.

Today, there are few landmarks named for the Catawba leader. But in the Anne Spring Close Greenway outside Fort Mill, SC — where Steele Creek turns into Sugar Creek — one of the area's prettiest spots is a trail around a man-made pond called Lake Haigler.

— Adapted and partially reprinted with permission from Rock Hill historian Louise Pettus

(continued from page 17)

Although he did not always succeed, Haigler (also spelled Hagler), known as Nopkehe among his own people [6], sought to balance relations between the Catawbas and settlers, and eventually negotiated a land deal with the English. In 1763, the English gave the Catawbas 144,000 acres near what is today Fort Mill and Rock Hill, SC as a reward for helping the English defeat the French in the French and Indian War. The land – which had once belonged to the Catawbas anyway – was the source of many problems in years to come.

In 1770, Samuel Davidson purchased a plot of land that became the site of Old Fort, NC. It remained a Westernmost outpost of Colonial civilization through 1776.

Near the Catawba River headwaters, the English and Cherokee were also busy negotiating similar land schemes. One early treaty stipulated that the British would settle no farther west than the crest of the Blue Ridge Mountains. Around 1770, Samuel Davidson purchased a plot of land that contained a stockade and is today the site of Old Fort, NC. Historians are still unsure who built the stockade (and even why it was built), but it remained the Westernmost outpost of Colonial civilization through 1776. After the American Revolution, German families began migrating down into the Catawba Valley from Pennsylvania and other northern areas that were too crowded.[7] The town of Morganton was established in 1784 as the site of a circuit court for the North Carolina frontier. The settlers built a post office in 1795 and an East/West road (now US 70) stretching from the Atlantic Ocean into Tennessee.

During this time, the Catawba River valley was sparsely settled; trade in forest and wildlife products were the primary means of commerce. Since farming and land use were minimal (there were no real commercial farms on the Catawba yet), land disturbance was relatively minimal and water quality across the entire Piedmont was excellent. In 1752 – as he explored western North Carolina in search of a location for a Moravian colony – Bishop Gottlieb Spangenberg described the upper tributaries of the Catawba as "crystal clear so that one can see the stones on the bottom even where the water is deep."[8]

Mount Dearborn near Great Falls, SC nearly became one of the nation's three armories. Remnants of this military outpost are still visible although the sensitive site is not yet open to the public.

But across the entire Piedmont Carolinas, the population density was increasing and many new settlers began moving from subsistence to commercial agriculture. Slowly, over the course of the next few decades and into the early 20th century, cotton and corn farming "all but irreparably gullied hundreds of thousands of acres of rich red hills and leached from the sand hills the little substance they possessed."[9]

Around the turn of the 19th century, several companies in South Carolina began investigating whether they could create a series of canals that would supplement the state's rivers and provide trade waterways from central North Carolina to the Atlantic at Georgetown and Charleston.[10] The Catawba Navigation Company proposed to connect the Catawba and Wateree rivers by cutting a canal to bypass the falls and shoals near Rocky Mount. This caught the ear of George Washington who nearly placed one of the nation's three armories on a 523-acre tract nearby. This site — known as Mount Dearborn near Great Falls, SC — remains one of the most interesting historical footnotes along the entire river. Today, Mount Dearborn is mostly local legend, its location known only to a few who are working to protect the archaeologically sensitive site.

In the late 1700s and early 1800s, the new Americans were still slowly spreading across the Piedmont. Trade routes were of paramount importance and the Catawba River — especially the area between Great Falls, SC and Charlotte, NC — played into those needs. In the period between 1820 and 1835, architect Robert Mills designed an elaborate series of canals intended to allow an alternate route around the shoals and rapids known as Land's Ford in Chester County, SC. The river, however, did not cooperate. Too high during floods and too low during drought, the canal proved undependable and was completely abandoned by 1840 once it became apparent that railroad transportation was far superior and more dependable. Today, the best-preserved remains exist at Landsford Canal State Park in South Carolina.

(continued to page 22)

"Plundering" Sam Brown: The Catawba Pirate?

Pirates may have been relatively common on the Carolina coast, but on the Catawba River they were few and far between — if they existed at all. But that doesn't mean various robbers and thieves ignored the area.

In fact, settlers in the Catawba River valley did fall victim to one particular rogue who took advantage of the lawless times during and after the Revolutionary War.

According to local history, a sinister Tory known as "Plundering" Sam Brown terrorized the area from Salisbury, NC on into York, SC during the 1780s. Brown led a loose band of robbers that included his own sister, Charity, stealing valuable items such as horses, pewterware, money and apparel.

Tradition has it that Brown married the daughter of a pioneer who lived near Island Ford. Unable to accept the life Brown led, she fled and returned home to her father. Brown later exacted his revenge by going to his father-in-law's home and killing all the man's stock. Brown was ultimately banished to southwestern North Carolina and was finally killed near the Tyger River in South Carolina after he threatened the wife of a brave — and armed — Whig settler.

More interesting than Brown's actual exploits, though, were tales of the supposed loot. According to local legend, Brown hid the spoils from his plundering trips in a cave at Lookout Shoals on the Catawba River. The cave was about three miles from the Island Ford, where a bluff on the western side of the Catawba River rose — at that time — more than 300 feet. A cave reportedly big enough to house several people opened about 60 feet from the base of this bluff under an overhanging cliff. Sometime later, apparently, the cave partially collapsed in a rockslide and today the river covers the whole area.

Many parties visited the area to search for the treasure, but it was never found. Folklore says that weird noises used to emanate from the cave when people approached it and that wind once blew down a large tree near the cave premises — spilling 12 sets of pewterware from its hollow trunk!

— Adapted and reprinted from A History of Catawba County, courtesy of Catawba Valley Historical Association

James Buchanan Duke (top) and Walker Gill Wylie (right) were among the first to tap into the Catawba's industrial possibilities.

(continued from page 20)

The upper Catawba, in particular, was fit more for mills than boats. One colonial surveyor noted that the "Wateree above (Great Falls) does not deserve the name river," alluding to colonial custom that only a boat-worthy stream would earn the designation as "river."[11] Even though local industrialists tried to clear the Catawba as far north as Beatty's Ford in Mecklenburg County, Lookout Shoals was thought to be the most formidable obstacle on the entire river and deterred any serious efforts.

On March 13, 1840, the small band of Indians that comprised the remaining Catawbas signed an agreement with the United States government known as the Treaty of Nation Ford. In this document, the Catawbas gave back their 144,000-acre reservation on the Catawba River — most of which had been leased out to settlers anyway — in exchange for a new tract of land in a less-populated area. The treaty proved disastrous for the Catawbas who now felt homeless and patently unwanted on a 630-acre reservation near the Catawba River. The Catawba Indians later explored living arrangements with the Cherokee in North Carolina and the Choctaw in Oklahoma, but both efforts failed and, by the early 1900s, the tribe was down to a few hundred members. The number would rise slowly for the next century as the Indians slowly resigned themselves to living on their small reservation in South Carolina.

The Catawba River remained a free-flowing part of the Piedmont landscape until the turn of the century. This was a difficult time in the South since in almost every aspect of modern life the reconstructing agricultural region lagged well behind the rest of a modernizing America. But by the late 19th century, textiles were rapidly emerging as the Piedmont's industry of the future and the Catawba River — with its seemingly unlimited potential for hydroelectric power — was ideally situated for the boom.

Two major events then set in motion a sea of change on the river and in the Carolinas. First, in 1899, James Buchanan Duke and partners organized the American Development Company to acquire land and water rights on the Catawba River in South Carolina. Then, in the summer of 1900, Dr. Walker Gill Wylie and his brother, Dr. Robert H. Wylie, incorporated the Catawba Power Company to build the

(continued to page 24)

The 'Sinking' of Fonta Flora

Historians who specialize in the mountains of North Carolina know many stories of communities that have simply disappeared over the years. Some early outposts fell during conflicts with Native American tribes while poor economic conditions claimed other mining towns and timber villages.

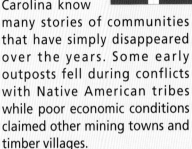

The Catawba River has similar stories to tell. One such tale is the town of Fonta Flora, named for the rich plant and animal life that once surrounded this tiny farming community at the base of Linville Gorge.

In the years leading up to the damming of Lake James, local companies began buying the rich farmland in between Marion and Morganton to make room for the lake. While much of this land was unpopulated, the citizens of Fonta Flora found themselves smack dab in the middle of the proposed lake project.

Established in the late 18th century by Irish immigrants, Fonta Flora grew slowly. It was a self-contained community with schoolhouse, store and churches, eventually earning a post office in 1870. After the Civil War, Fonta Flora became a resettlement community for freed slaves. According to The Charlotte Observer, many of these folks sharecropped with white farmers and the community soon had several merchants, stores, homes and the oldest black church in Burke County.

Everything began to change around 1915 when residents — in need of a power supply — began selling their land to Western Carolina Power Company. Soon most of the community had moved away and the waters of the Catawba and Linville Rivers slowly rose to cover the buildings.

Residents recall visiting the lake in years past and gazing down into the clear water at structures now submerged under 40 feet of water.

"You could see old standing chimneys and houses," local historian Nettie McIntosh told the Rock Hill Herald in 2001. "They didn't move anything when they built the dam. Part of the old cemetery is still there."

– Sources include
The Charlotte Observer
(May 7, 2000), USGenWeb and
The Rock Hill Herald *(July 4, 2001)*

(continued from page 22)

Catawba Hydro Station near Rock Hill, SC. A New York physician who grew up near Chester, SC, Walker Gill Wylie was one of the first to envision a hydroelectric power system on the Catawba River, later proclaiming it, "with the exception of the Penobscot River [in Maine], the best river east of the Rockies for power development."[12]

In 1904, the Catawba Power Company completed the Catawba Hydro Station on the river in York, SC – this is widely considered the birth date of Duke Power. For the next century, the history of the Catawba River and Duke Power is intertwined and, far too detailed to document here. (Robert F. Durden's *Electrifying the Piedmont Carolinas* and Joe Maynor's *Duke Power, the first 75 years* offer thorough histories of the power company; Thomas Wyche offers a summary of Duke's land conservation record in his book, *Mosaic*.) Suffice to say that the Wylie brothers, J.B. Duke, William States Lee and others quickly bought into the opportunity for multiple, interconnected hydroelectric plants along the Catawba. Their vision was for a reliable and efficient system that could literally pump life into a growing region.

In North Carolina's mountain region, the power company was slower to tap into the Catawba River's bounty. This area was already a draw for tourists. Railroads such as Western North Carolina Railroad and Southern Railway Company were building many lines across and around the Catawba intended for both industry and travel. Hickory was fast becoming a major furniture and manufacturing town while in Old Fort, the Union Tanning Company, begun in 1904, became one of the region's dominant industries. The company's tannery was fed with wood by a flume running down from the headwaters of Curtis Creek and also a narrow gauge railroad running from Catawba Falls.

By 1916, Duke Power had completed four hydro stations on the Catawba River and many railroad

The Catawba at flood stage (top) and water pouring over the spillway (right) at Lookout Dam during the disastrous flood of 1940.

Traveling musicians like the ones here (top) occasionally entertained construction workers at Duke's hydro stations. Once the Great Falls Reservoir was built in 1923, boating became a popular pastime (right).

PHOTOS COURTESY DUKE POWER

bridges and roads were built elsewhere. For industrialists and workers, everything seemed to be going well. But disaster struck in July 1916 when unprecedented rainfall from two separate storm systems wreaked havoc along the entire river.[13] Heavy rains early in the month had already saturated the ground, but then a cyclone dumped *19 inches* of rain on July 15 and 16. The ensuing flood knocked out many of the fledgling power company's plants and caused millions of dollars of damage.

After a lengthy cleanup, Duke's response to this flood was unique. The company decided to build a series of three interlinked dams on the headwaters of the Catawba and create a vast reservoir behind the dams.[14] The creation of Lake James — which was intended in part to prevent future floods — was also another huge step toward a reliable and interconnected system of hydroelectric plants.

After the 1916 incident, a new hydro station opened every few years for the next decade. Fishing Creek (1916) opened first, followed by Bridgewater at Lake James (1919), Dearborn at the Great Falls Reservoir (1923), Mountain Island (1923), Rhodhiss (1925), Cedar Creek (1926) and Oxford at Lake Hickory (1928). Although engineers believed the dams might prevent another flood of Biblical proportions, Mother Nature was not so cooperative. In 1940 an even more damaging flood overwhelmed dams up and down the river, causing millions of dollars in damage and turning many bridges into twisted heaps of metal. Residents all along the river, once again, went into recovery mode.

Floods aside, the early 20th century was a difficult period on the Catawba River. As Southern culture gradually transitioned from single-

Spiderwort

family farms to fewer, larger farms — with many supplying "green gold" to the timber industry — the erosion of Piedmont lands began far outpacing the river's capacity to restore it. As far back as the early 1880s, a survey for potential water power in the Catawba River area of South Carolina found that its streams were "in many places filling up with detritus, sand and mud, which is washed in from hillsides so that many shoals are being rapidly obliterated, and at many places where, within memory of middle-aged men, there were shoals or falls of five to 10 feet, at present scarcely any shoals can be noticed."[15] Cotton and corn culture dictated maximum use of acreage and the resultant clearing operations dumped red Piedmont clay into the Catawba at unprecedented levels. In the geologic blink of an eye, the river turned murky and silt-laden, smothering aquatic plants and killing the game fish that depended on sight for prey. Weakened by this excess turbidity, the Catawba was in no state to cope with additional burdens in the form of raw sewage from fast-growing Piedmont towns and the industrial wastes of the region's early cotton finishing plants.[16] But, spearheaded by the Soil Conservation Service, modern farming practices slowly helped address this trend. At the same time, Duke's new power plants also played a role in the recovery. The still waters of the vast lakes allowed much of the silt to settle and the biological processes that take place in lakes enhanced the Catawba's ability to absorb its growing industrial and municipal pollution load.[17]

After World War II, the growth of water-dependent industry posed another serious threat to the river's health. Although the Carolinas benefited from more than 2,500 new industries, 400,000 new jobs and $6 billion in investment in the 1950s, many of these new companies needed the Catawba in some fashion or another. Industries such as Springs Industries (textiles) and Bowater (pulp and paper mills) boomed but also required huge volumes of water both to run their operations and remove waste. Considering period technology, a single textile finishing plant could produce the pollution burden of a city of 100,000 people.[18] In the South Carolina Piedmont, for instance, Springs provides jobs for some 5,000 people because it maintained the nation's largest dyeing operation under one roof — the Grace

Bleachery. Other local industries in modern times include the Duracell battery plant, which produces almost a billion AA batteries a year!

Meanwhile, Duke's power plant construction on the Catawba River had involved new coal fired stations until, in 1957, it announced a plan to build Cowans Ford Dam and Hydro Station northwest of Charlotte. This was the last such project feasible on the Catawba and certainly the company's biggest to date. Building the dam and planning for the lake involved a massive land-clearing operation and thrust Duke headlong into the real estate business. In 1969, the company created a subsidiary, Crescent Land and Timber, first to manage the timber, then eventually its real estate holdings. If Duke's engineers saw the dam and Lake Norman primarily as a reservoir of cooling water for its steam plants, local residents saw something else: a huge new recreational asset.[19] While important from a purely economic point of view, the creation of Lake Norman was also an awakening of sorts, leading many people up and down the Catawba to see the "river" in a different light.

Legislation in both Carolinas had been addressing pollution issues for several years but, in 1972, the Clean Water Act added an exclamation point to the decade-long effort to resuscitate the Catawba. Today, the river remains a key to continued growth and tourism in the Piedmont while the natural areas along the Catawba River are developing as they have for thousands of years — albeit in closer proximity to man. Few places in the Carolinas can boast the dual distinction of great diversity and understudied resource. But, as the next section indicates, naturalists who study the Catawba River are discovering a new fascination with the valley on an ongoing and continuous basis.

A great blue heron enjoys its catch on the Catawba River.

Naturally Catawba: flora & fauna

With everything from high country black bear habitat in the Blue Ridge Mountains to spotted salamanders in the wetlands near Landsford Canal, the Catawba River basin is literally teeming with flowers, fish, reptiles, wading birds and mammals. If we were to consider the entire river basin, we could also discuss ecosystems from mountains to sea. Most of us, however, consider the Catawba a "Piedmont" river.

Although Carolinians like to claim this area as our own, the Piedmont (the word means "foot of the mountain") is actually a vast physiographic providence that stretches southwest to northeast from Alabama to New York. The Piedmont drops gradually from an elevation of around 1,500 feet near the Blue Ridge to about 500 feet at the fall line, the point at which the Catawba begins cutting across hard upland rocks and into the softer sediment of the Coastal plain. Before man settled here, the Piedmont's natural diversity was extraordinary and encompassed ecological regions we wouldn't normally associate with this area.

> **...the Catawba River and its banks provide habitat for more than 50 species of fish, 206 species of birds and 120 species of trees.**

For instance, in their early travels of the area, explorers from de Soto to English-born John Lawson reported many *prairies* – including one near Salisbury, NC that was 25 miles across! Piedmont prairies were not as large as those in the Midwest because the many creeks and rivers created natural breaks, but they were certainly a prominent part of the landscape when Europeans arrived. While it's possible that thousands of years of farming and burning by Native Americans could have created some of these prairies, the Piedmont nonetheless provided a home for a thriving population of buffalo and prairie grasses such as Indian grass and switch grass. Today, the region's most acclaimed prairie plant is Schweinitz's sunflower, a species so rare it was designated federally endangered in 1991 (see page 30). It is possible to view several prairies in the process of being restored at Latta Plantation Nature Preserve and McDowell Nature Preserve near Charlotte. In the vicinity of Rock Hill, SC, the South Carolina Department of Natural Resources manages the Blackjacks Heritage Preserve, which contains areas of prairie that are also protected.

Now that the area is so densely populated it is sometimes hard to visualize the Piedmont as a "natural" home for anything other than people, malls and roads. But the Catawba River and its banks provide habitat for more than 50 species of fish, 206 species of birds and 120 species of trees. We've detailed just a few of these species here, although this is by no means a comprehensive list. You can learn more by contacting organizations such as the Katawba Valley Land Trust or check the appendix for additional resources.

FLORA — Trees and Shrubs

The banks of the Catawba River include a number of diverse natural areas and many types of spectacular native trees. At Lake James, for instance, the primary tree cover is a mix of hardwoods with white pines and Eastern hemlocks dominating the landscape. By the time the Catawba has made its way to Lake Norman, the river is surrounded by mid-successional forest with tulip poplar, hickory, sweet gum and small shrubs. Further down at Landsford Canal, bottomland stream forests offer habitat for oak, hickory and ash.

Although it is typically not found in South Carolina, the big leaf magnolia is one of the most interesting trees found along the South Fork in Gaston County, NC. This 35-foot tree blooms in May and June with a gorgeous, cupped white flower. This tree has the largest simple leaf (to 32 inches) and flower (to 10 inches in diameter) of any tree native to

Leave No Trace

▲ Plan ahead and prepare: know regulations and concerns for the area you visit. Prepare for weather and hazards.

▲ Travel and camp on durable surfaces: use established trails and campsites. Consider impact at all times.

▲ Dispose of waste properly: pack it in; pack it out.

▲ Leave what you find: preserve the past and all natural objects.

▲ Minimize campfire impacts: keep fires small and use established rings or pans.

▲ Respect wildlife: observe from a distance and never feed animals.

▲ Be considerate of other visitors: respect other visitors and protect the quality of their experience.

Visit www.lnt.org for more information.

Hardwoods show fall colors on Mountain Island Lake.

the United States. Conservation groups along the river corridor will occasionally lead trips to explore these trees. More common along the river are river birch, sycamore and white oak. Some other common species of trees include:

▲ **Eastern white pine:** The largest conifer in Eastern North America, these trees commonly reach 100 feet in height and four feet in diameter. The tree has soft, bluish-green needles three to five inches long that remain on the tree for several years. It is restricted primarily to the upper reaches of the Catawba River.

▲ **Red maple:** This tree is common across the Carolinas and may grow to be 115 feet tall, although it more commonly reaches 40 to 70 feet. In autumn the maple's leaves turn brilliant scarlet and yellow.

▲ **White ash:** Found in both bottomland and upland hardwood forests, the stout white ash grows to around 90 feet in height. The tree's crown is usually rounded and its bark is a deep brown to gray with many fissures.

FLORA —
Wildflowers

The Catawba River valley has an abundant supply of common wildflowers; so many, in fact, that it's hard to find a comprehensive list!

PHOTO COURTESY OF MECKLENBURG COUNTY.

Schweinitz's sunflower was designated federally endangered in 1991. It is still found in some places near the Catawba River.

Because of its relatively mild climate, the Catawba also offers year-round viewing with species blooming every month of the year along much of the river. Some of the best viewing areas include Linville Gorge, the Catawba River Greenway, Lake Norman State Park, Latta Plantation Nature Preserve and Landsford Canal State Park. Among the most common wildflowers found in the Catawba area are butterfly weed (small, brilliant orange flowers that emerge in dry fields from June through August), dwarf crested iris (deep purple flowers found in open woods during March and April) and Indian pipe (a single white drooping flower found in moist shaded woods during late summer and fall).

A few wildflowers in the Catawba River area warrant special attention:

▲ **Schweinitz's Sunflower:** Found only in the rare, dry areas that resemble Piedmont prairies, this plant erupts in yellow petals during September and October and – to this point – has only been found within a 50-mile radius of Charlotte. The sunflower once thrived along rail lines in this area where sparks from the coal-fired engines commonly caused fires in the woods. It is now best viewed in county parks and nature preserves of Mountain Island Lake and Lake Wylie.

At night, it is common to hear – and occasionally see – mammals such as this playful raccoon.

▲ **Rocky Shoals Spider Lily:** This two-foot tall lily is not an imperiled species, but it is increasingly rare in the Piedmont. The flowers are found only along rocky rivers in Alabama, South Carolina and Georgia. At Landsford Canal State Park, the flower seems to blanket every dry spot on the shoals during peak season and an annual event, Lily Fest, takes place each May to celebrate the display.

▲ **Lady's Slipper:** This wild orchid includes both pink and yellow species. The pink species is commonly found in dry forests but the yellow is threatened in many states and very rare in the Piedmont.

FAUNA —
Mammals, Songbirds, Raptors and Wading Birds

The Catawba River is home to an amazing variety of mammals spanning from the ordinary to the not so common. In North Carolina's mountains, visitors to the Catawba North Fork commonly paddle past dams built by playful beavers or hear the nighttime exploits of raccoon and fox. But most of the mammals in the Catawba Valley are solitary types and best viewed at one of the area's many nature centers. Many visitors to Linville Caverns go just to view the tiny Eastern Pipistrelle bat, which hibernates there during the winter months. Some notable mammals in the Catawba River corridor include:

▲ **River otters, muskrat and mink:** There are three fur-bearing species along the riverbank area. Muskrat and mink are common, and river otter sightings in the Catawba River area are on the rise thanks to a reintroduction project by the North Carolina Wildlife Resources Commission.

10 Outdoor Trip Essentials

1. Adequate water and food
2. Trail or topographic map
3. Compass
4. Adequate clothing (this may include rain gear or sunglasses)
5. Knife
6. First-aid kit
7. Headlamp or flashlight
8. Waterproof matches
9. Signaling device (whistle or mirror)
10. Insect repellent

▲ **Black bear:** These shy and reclusive animals avoid human contact at almost all cost, preferring to root for food in wild areas such as Linville Gorge or the Catawba's headwaters near Curtis Creek. Bears prefer to forage for food in oak, hickory and mixed hardwood forests with blueberry and huckleberry thickets.

If bird watching is on your agenda during a trip to the Catawba, you're in luck. In Mecklenburg County — the heart of the Catawba River valley — naturalists have identified some 283 species of birds and the local Audubon Society is one of the most active such groups in the region. (Not all the birds live on the Catawba; see appendix for additional information.) The Mountain Island Lake area of the river was designated one of the first three Important Bird Areas in North Carolina. On the Catawba River in South Carolina — where the water is free flowing for more than 30 miles — it is common to view raptors such as the bald eagle, osprey and red-tailed hawks. Some notable raptors in the Catawba River area include:

▲ **Bald Eagle:** These majestic birds are relatively common sights today at Landsford Canal State Park and several undisclosed nesting sites around Lake James. Although it is no longer endangered, the bald eagle is still threatened by development in some places.

▲ **Osprey:** The "fish hawk," as it is also known, hunts for fish along the low shorelines of all of the lakes and free-flowing sections of the Catawba. The best time to view these birds are in the spring and fall, when it is also possible to watch them building stick nests in dead trees or on river buoys.

▲ **Owls:** These nocturnal birds — primarily screech, great horned and barred owls — are quite common along the Catawba River. The best way to observe them is during a visit to the Carolina Raptor Center.

Wading and diving birds such as great blue heron, egrets and kingfishers are some of the biggest natural attractions along the entire Catawba River, especially at publicly accessible areas such as Cowans Ford Wildlife Refuge and Lake Norman State Park. Water birds such as loons, horned grebes and Bonaparte's gulls can be seen across Lake Norman, but the best time for birding here is winter since there aren't as many boats on the water. Problem is, you'll need a boat yourself in many areas since there is very little unoccupied shoreline! However, there are some excellent places to observe wading birds without a boat. These include the Fort Mill Access Area below the Lake Wylie dam, the Lugoff Access Area below the Wateree dam and Landsford Canal State Park. These areas provide great viewing for wading birds such as heron, great egrets and snowy egrets. Raptors are also common in these areas including bald eagles, red-shouldered hawks and ospreys. One of the most notable wading birds is:

▲ **Great Blue Heron:** In 2000, scientists observed more than 30 active nests at a great blue heron rookery on an island in Lake Norman. Some say these birds are no longer "notable" since they have grown so common in the Southeast, but it's hard not to be impressed when you see one take flight using its five-foot wing span.

FAUNA — Amphibians, Reptiles and Fish

Slippery, slithery and crawling creatures don't garner the type of romantic attention usually reserved for osprey or black bear. But while they are often overlooked, amphibians and reptiles are important components of Catawba River ecosystems. Herpetologists have recorded 32 species of reptiles and 17 species of amphibians in the Landsford Canal area alone. In North Carolina, both mountain and Piedmont regions offer habitat for salamanders, turtles, snakes, tree frogs and lizards.

The fishing, as one would expect, is excellent along the entire Catawba River. Gamefish such as largemouth bass, crappie, bluegill and catfish are common up and down the river while walleye and smallmouth bass occur in the headwater reservoirs (see Fishing, page 105 for more information). One notable amphibian of the Catawba River is the "Spotless" spotted salamander.

A northern banded water snake with a catfish in its mouth.

Catawba Falls

Lake James

Lake James, at the confluence of the Catawba and Linville Rivers, boasts 6,510 acres of surface area in the foothills of McDowell and Burke counties. Recreational opportunities abound on its clear waters and along its 150 miles of shoreline. Largely undeveloped, Lake James hugs the Pisgah National Forest, providing riparian habitats for diverse plant and animal species, as well as quiet coves for fishing and recreation. Lake James State Park straddles the county line along the lake's southern shores and offers a variety of outdoor interests.

Location

Lake James lies just north of Interstate 40 and along the eastern edge of Pisgah National Forest in McDowell and Burke counties, NC.

Recreation: Paddling, Biking and Fishing

The setting of Lake James, resting at the base of the Appalachian Mountains, calls to the spirit of outdoor enthusiasts. Traditional water sports include canoeing, kayaking and recreational boating. Some of the state's record-breaking fish were caught in the numerous backwater coves. Hiking, biking, picnicking and camping opportunities abound along stretches of pristine shoreline. Flora and fauna thrive in wetland habitats and present wondrous displays for wildlife observers.

Just east of Lake James and below the Linville Dam, the **Bridgewater Fishing Area and Canoe Access** offers access to a gorgeous, free-flowing section of the Catawba River. One local outfitter, **CBS Sports** in Morganton, offers a four-hour guided canoe trip from this access to the Catawba River Greenway. The trip includes a guide, life vests, canoes and transportation. For information, visit CBS Sports at 911 N. Green Street in Morganton or call (828) 437-7016.

Lake James Landing is a full-service camping and recreation facility on Lake James. Canoe rentals are available by calling (828) 652-2907.

Considering its mountain setting at the base of Pisgah National Forest, Lake James also offers some of the best bicycling in the region — both in the form of mountain biking trails and on-road cycling. **Lake James Road** is a designated bike route that winds around the perimeter of Lake James. Occasional views of the lake greet riders as they travel in and out of wooded areas. Connecting with NC 126, riders can cross the lake and travel through Lake James State Park or use this route as a "base" from which to organize trips.

Lakeside Camping and Nearby Bed & Breakfasts

There are numerous camping facilities, hotels, motels and other lodging opportunities near the Catawba River. This list primarily includes riverside camping opportunities or Bed & Breakfasts. These inns provide a comfortable alternative to camping, and allow visitors to experience the sights and recreation of the river in a multi-day experience.

(continued to page 37)

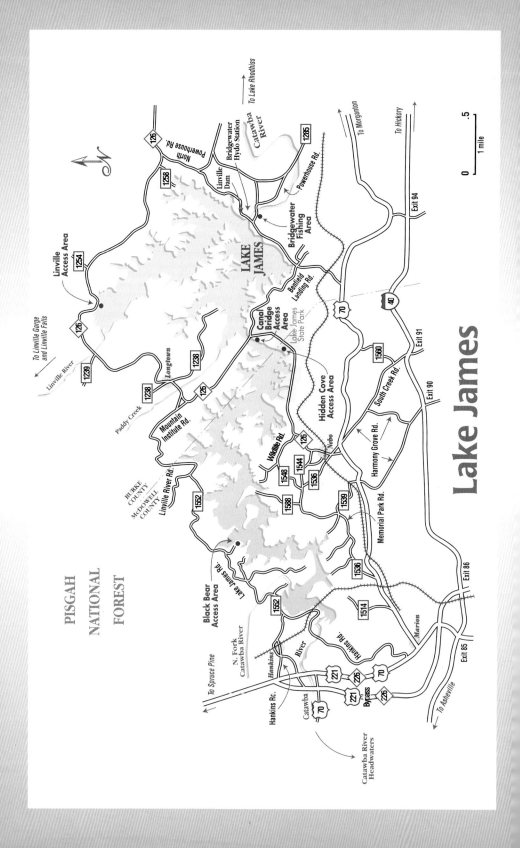

Lake James

(continued from page 35)

Catawba Falls Campground: 18 full hookup sites, 9 electric-only sites, 17 tent sites and one rental cabin. Almost all sites are on the Catawba River. Information: 35 Peggy Loop, off Catawba River Road, (828) 668-4831.

Lake James Landing and Campground: Full-service camp-sites, cabin rentals, boat ramps and storage, boat and canoe rentals, fishing supplies and a convenience store. Information: Lake James Road, west side of lake, (828) 652-2907.

Lake James Family Campground: 120 full-service sites on Lake James. Boat ramp on-site and convenience store nearby. Information: 10 miles west of Morganton, 4 miles off Interstate 40 on Benfield Landing Road, (828) 584-0190.

Lake James State Park: 20 backpack sites available, 2 designated hand-icapped, with fireplace, grill and picnic tables. Water locations are throughout the campground and a washhouse with hot showers is on-site. Information: (see page 39 for park details) located on US 126, Nebo, NC.

Rose Creek Campground: 72 full-service sites and 18 tent sites near the Catawba River above Lake Rhodhiss. Swimming, fishing, game room, camper sales and service. Information: 3471 Rose Creek Road, Morganton, NC, (828) 438-4338.

The Inn at Blue Ridge: This inn, located within the Blue Ridge Country Club, features 12 rooms with stone fireplaces and balconies overlooking the North Fork of the Catawba River. Rooms include continental breakfast. Additionally, there are 3-bedroom town homes available. Information: 17677 US Hwy. 221 N, Marion, NC, (828) 756-7001.

Festivals and Events

Earth Day at Lake James State Park — April: Lake James State Park holds a number of annual events including this celebration in April. Booths and displays educate and entertain on topics such as water quality, wildlife, natural environ-ments and forestry. Information: (828) 652-5047.

Mountain Glory Festival — October: The City of Marion sponsors the Mountain Glory Festival annually on the second Saturday in October. This all-day street festival gives visitors an opportunity to view and purchase works from dozens of artists and crafters. Music, chil-dren's areas, bike and foot races are all part of this event. A large number of food vendors keep the crowds from getting hungry. Information: (828) 652-3551.

Destinations: Lake James State Park

Established in 1987, this popular park includes 565 acres on the southern shores of Lake James near Marion, NC. The park offers two boating access ramps, one of which (Canal Bridge) is open 24 hours. There are 20 tent camping sites with fire pits, grills, tables and water avail-able. Hiking trails wind through the park and lead to scenic overlooks.

(continued to page 39)

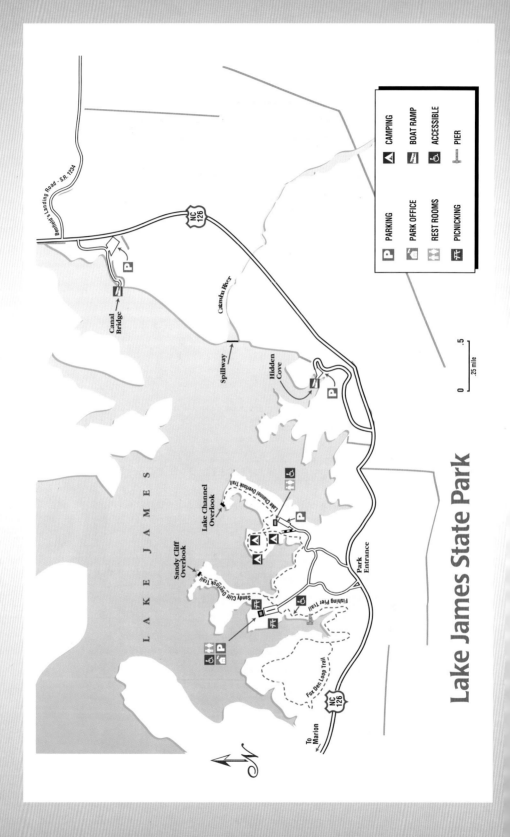

Lake James State Park

LEGEND

P	PARKING	◢	CAMPING
	PARK OFFICE		BOAT RAMP
	REST ROOMS		ACCESSIBLE
⨎	PICNICKING		PIER

Benjab's Landing Road - S.R. 1234

NC 126

Canal Bridge

Catawba River

Spillway

Hidden Cove

LAKE JAMES

Lake Channel Overlook

Lake Channel Overlook Trail

Sandy Cliff Overlook

Sandy Cliff Overlook Trail

Fishing Pier Trail

Park Entrance

Fox Den Loop Trail

NC 126

To Marion

0   .25 mile   .5

N

(continued from page 37)

A picnic area and shelter is located on the shoreline of the lake and a swimming beach with refreshment stand is near the park office.

Location and park hours: Take Exit 90 off Interstate 40 and head north across US 70. Follow signs to the park entrance. The park opens daily at 8 a.m. year-round, and the park office operates Monday to Friday from 8 a.m. to 5 p.m.

The North Carolina Division of Parks and Recreation does not charge entrance fees for its parks. Costs in the parks are associated with use of certain facilities such as boat rentals, camping, swimming and cabins. Fees range from $3 to rent a canoe, $8 for primitive campsites and $20 for picnic shelter reservations.

Things to do: Whether you're interested in sport fishing, interpretive programs or trail running, Lake James State Park has it all. Cool, deep lake water coupled with warm surface temperature help make largemouth and smallmouth bass the most sought-after fish at the lake. Most park officials will tell you spring through fall is the best season for fishing, especially when you're trying in early morning or late afternoon.

The trails at Lake James State Park aren't necessarily long, but they offer a nice variety for outdoor enthusiasts such as trail runners. By combining trails such as the Fox Den Loop (2.2 miles) with the Sandy Cliff Overlook (1.5 miles) your views span from the sheer cliffs of Shortoff Mountain towering over Linville Gorge to a dense lakeshore forest teeming with wildflowers, white pines and rhododendron.

The picnic area at Lake James includes both a large shelter with tables for group gatherings (free of charge unless you need to make a reservation) and 20 individual sites with outdoor grills.

For more information: Lake James State Park, PO Box 340, Nebo, NC 28761. Call (828) 652-5047. Visit the North Carolina Division of Parks and Recreation web site (see appendix) for details.

Destinations: Linville Gorge

The Linville Gorge Wilderness Area dominates the landscape in North Carolina's "high country" — a mountainous region in the northwestern section of the state. A 14-mile canyon cleaved by the Linville River, the gorge is formed by Linville Mountain on the west and Jonas Ridge on the east. (The Linville River crashes down this narrow gorge until it becomes part of the Catawba at Lake James.) It is a spectacularly wild area that features many miles of hiking trails, backcountry camping and a jumble of fractured and hard-to-reach cliffs.

Location: The North Carolina high country is a maze of roads. Main arteries such as the Blue Ridge Parkway, US 221, US 321 and NC 181 slice through these mountains, but there are numerous smaller state and county roads that could either make your trip shorter or dead-end at a gated community. There are accesses to the wilderness area on both the east and west rims of Linville Gorge.

For the east rim of Linville Gorge and Table Rock Picnic Area: From Charlotte, follow Interstate 40 to Exit

105 in Morganton (NC 18). Follow NC 18 north through Morganton for two miles until it turns into NC 181. Continue another 23 miles on NC 181 to turn left (west) onto Gingercake Road (SR-1264) at a sign for the Linville Gorge Wilderness Area and the Table Rock Picnic Area. At 0.3 miles veer left onto the first fork, Table Rock Road (SR-1261). Shortly this becomes FR-210, which is a dirt road. Follow 8.5 miles to Table Rock Picnic Area.

For the west rim and Linville Gorge Information Cabin: From Asheville, follow Interstate 40 to Exit 72 for US 70 and Old Fort. Follow US 70 east to Marion. In Marion, turn left onto US 221 heading north for Linville. Follow US 221 to Linville and turn right onto NC 183 heading east. After about 0.2 miles on NC 183, you will pass a right turn for Kistler Memorial Highway (which is actually a dirt road and not recommended for two-wheel drive vehicles) and the western rim of Linville Gorge. Follow this dirt road a short distance to the Information Cabin, which is open 9 a.m. to 5 p.m. seven days a week. Pick up a camping permit here if needed.

Things to do: Overnight camping trips are extremely popular in Linville Gorge. Permits are required for camping only on weekends and holidays during the period of May 1 through October 31. Permits are not required for visitors who do not stay overnight. You can obtain these free permits by contacting the District Ranger's Office in Nebo, NC from Monday through Friday, 8 a.m. to 4:30 p.m. Walk-in permits, for the current week only, are available at the Linville Gorge Information Cabin.

Free camping is available along FR-210 en route to the Table Rock Picnic Area and there are many flat, shady spots available for tent camping on the trail toward The Chimneys. Do not camp in the Table Rock Picnic Area parking lot.

There are more than 39 miles of trail in Linville Gorge, from popular, easy walks to areas such as The Chimneys to serious backcountry endeavors like the Jonas Ridge or Rock Jock Trails. North Carolina's Mountains-to-Sea Trail, which connects Table Rock and Shortoff Mountain on the gorge's east rim, is an extremely popular outing. The gorge is lined with large quartzite cliffs up to 500 feet in height, which provide dramatic views from either rim.

For more information: Pisgah National Forest−Grandfather Ranger District, 109 East Lawing Drive, Nebo, NC 29761, (828) 652-2144. The office is nine miles east of Marion, NC off Interstate 40 and Exit 90 (for Lake James/Nebo).

Shortoff Mountain − seen here in the distance − towers over Linville Gorge and provides a gorgeous backdrop to Lake James.

Day Trips: Catawba Waterfalls

There was a time when the Catawba River flowed free and unobstructed – at least by anything man-made. The river had to negotiate changes in topography, islands, shoals and plunges all on its own. Today, many of those sites, where abrupt changes in elevation created waterfalls along the river, are the locations of the dams that create the power supply our modern world demands. However, few and far between, we can still find spots that testify to the once-wild state of the Catawba River.

CATAWBA FALLS

Perhaps it is appropriate that the Catawba should begin its long journey with a spectacular waterfall. Catawba Falls is a 70-foot plunge not far from the headwaters of the Catawba River near Old Fort, NC.

Directions: To get there, take Exit 73 from Interstate 40. Turn left, go under the interstate and immediately turn right. At the fork, bear left onto Catawba River Road and travel to the end. Park on the shoulder, find trail across bridge and to the right.

Hours: Permission from the landowner is required.

For more information: Contact Catawba Falls Campground, (828) 668-4831.

LINVILLE FALLS

Linville Falls is one of the most celebrated waterfalls in the southeast. Located along the Linville River, which joins the Catawba River at

Linville Falls cascades 120 feet into the Linville River.

Lake James, the falls cut through sheer cliffs and cascade 120 feet into the scenic Linville Gorge. The falls are accessible by a number of hiking trails and are a popular destination for visitors to the Linville Gorge Wilderness Area.

Directions: To get there, leave the Blue Ridge Parkway at milepost 316.5 and continue 1.4 miles to the parking lot. The falls can also be reached from a parking lot near the village of Linville Falls, NC.

Hours: The trails to Linville Falls are open year-round, but most facilities close during the winter months.

For more information: Visit the National Park Service online (see appendix).

Fishing on the Catawba River just upstream of Lake Rhodhiss.

Lake Rhodhiss, Lake Hickory, Lookout Shoals Lake

Lake Rhodhiss is a long, narrow body of water; a widening of the Catawba River held at bay by the Rhodhiss Dam. With 3,060 acres of surface area and 90 miles of shoreline, Lake Rhodhiss is a relatively small neighbor to Lake James. Flowing toward the eastern border of Burke County, Lake Rhodhiss becomes the boundary between Burke and Caldwell counties.

Lake Hickory picks up where Rhodhiss leaves off, forcing the Catawba to widen again as it continues eastward. Three additional tributaries contribute to Lake Hickory before the Oxford Dam holds the waters back. Lake Hickory is slightly bigger than Rhodhiss at 4,223 acres of surface area and 105 miles of shoreline, and shares boundaries with Caldwell, Alexander and Catawba counties.

Beyond Oxford Dam, the succession of lakes that is the Catawba turns southward as they are joined by the Lower Little River. This elbow of water is Lookout Shoals Lake. The lake manages to accumulate 1,305 acres of surface area and 37 miles of shoreline before it pushes against the Lookout Shoals Dam. The three reservoirs act not only as important sources of electric generation, but also as recreational outlets for outdoor enthusiasts. Popular among local sportspeople, Lakes Rhodhiss, Hickory and Lookout Shoals offer some of the finest fishing opportunities in the state.

Location

Lake Rhodhiss and Lake Hickory are north of Interstate 40, stretching east from Morganton and passing Granite Falls and Hickory before turning south at Lookout Shoals Lake.

Recreation: Paddling, Biking and Fishing

Lake Hickory, the largest of the three lakes, offers the most public boating access areas as well as a number of marinas. For canoeing, fishing and picnicking, Catawba County's River Bend Park and the City of Hickory's Glen C. Hilton Park and John Geitner Park provides additional lakeside opportunities. A bank fishing area is also located in Burke County on Lake Rhodhiss.

Canoe accesses are plentiful along this three-lake chain and two of the most convenient put-ins are at the **Catawba River Greenway** in Morganton (see map page 44). This 272-acre greenway runs for more than a mile along the Catawba between Lake James and Lake Rhodhiss. It offers canoe and kayak put-in and take-out points. The park — which is filled with Carolina silverbell, sycamore, blackgum and two dozen other species of Piedmont trees — also includes a paved walking and biking trail, a multi-level observation deck and a 170-foot bridge crossing Silver Creek. With its picnic shelters and open tables near a gazebo and playground, this is one of the nicest spots around for an afternoon picnic. The *Catawba River Tree Identification Guide* is available at a kiosk near the park entrance. The Catawba River Greenway is located just off US 70 in Morganton. For more information: (828) 437-8863.

(continued to page 45)

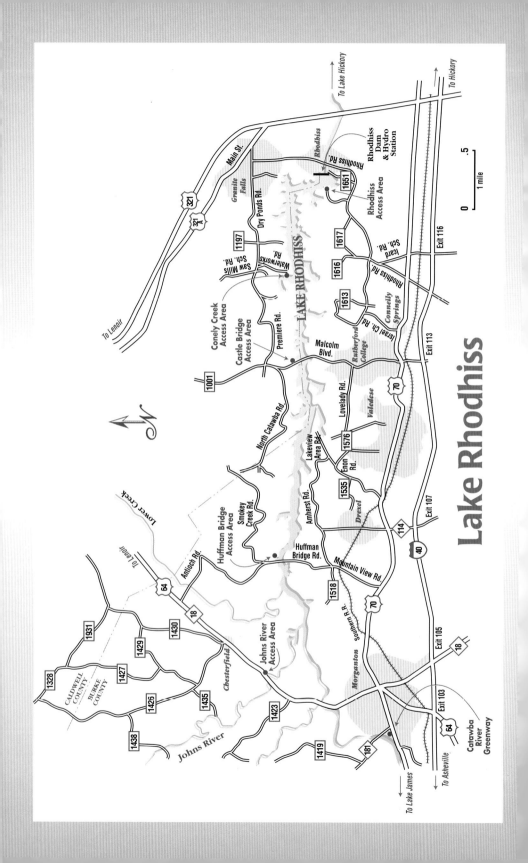

Lake Rhodhiss

(continued from page 43)

Glenn C. Hilton Park on Lake Hickory offers a boat access as well as trails and picnic areas. The hiking and walking trails offer easy strolling for young families or those who just want to take it easy. The greenway boardwalk, observation deck and butterfly gardens add to the scenic values of this park. Visitors can also use picnic shelters with tables and grills, a gazebo, volleyball courts and horseshoe pits. Hilton Park is located at 2000 6th Street in Hickory (see map page 46).

Hickory's other popular lakeside destination is **John Geitner Park** on the east side of US 321 on Lake Hickory. This greenway offers picnic shelters with tables and grills, a gazebo and nature trail. As part of the City of Hickory's greenway project, the paved 1.5-mile trail in this park also links to Hickory City Park. An additional 2.4 miles of mountain bike trails are also accessed by this bikeway. Geitner Park's boat ramp, fishing area and picnic facilities make this a popular recreation spot. Future trails will be added to link a third park to the bikeway. Geitner Park is located at 2035 12th Street in Hickory (see map page 46).

For more information about both lakeside parks in Hickory, call (828) 322-7046 or visit the city's web page (see appendix).

Lakeside Camping and Nearby Bed & Breakfasts

There are numerous camping facilities, hotels, motels and other lodging opportunities near the Catawba River. This list primarily includes riverside camping opportunities or Bed & Breakfasts. These inns provide a comfortable alternative to camping, and allow visitors to experience the sights and recreation of the river in a multi-day experience.

Rose Creek Campground: 72 full-service sites and 18 tent sites near the Catawba River above Lake Rhodhiss. Swimming, fishing, game room, camper sales and service. Information: 3471 Rose Creek Road, Morganton, NC, (828) 438-4338.

Lake Hickory RV Resort: 200 seasonal sites with 10 to 12 available for nightly use. On the lake with boat ramp, marina, picnic pavilion, mini-golf and boardwalk. Information: 6641 Monford Drive, Conover, NC, (828) 256-4303.

Fairway Oaks Bed and Breakfast: This farmhouse-style inn is located on the Silver Creek Plantation Golf Course, five miles from downtown Morganton, NC. Four rooms and a gathering room are available to visitors, as well as a garden, gazebo and 1.7-mile walking trail through the golf course. Information: 4640 Plantation Drive, Morganton, NC. (828) 584-7677 or (877) 584 7611.

Halle House Bed and Breakfast: The Halle House is located in Granite Falls, NC, with easy access to Lake Rhodhiss and Lake Hickory. Built in 1920, it offers three guest rooms with private baths. The porches overlook 3.5 acres with a goldfish pond. Information: 25 Hillside Avenue, Granite Falls, NC, (828) 313-3989 or (888) 256-0745.

The Hickory Bed and Breakfast: This inn is located in Hickory, NC, convenient to shopping and lake activities, and offers four guest

(continued to page 47)

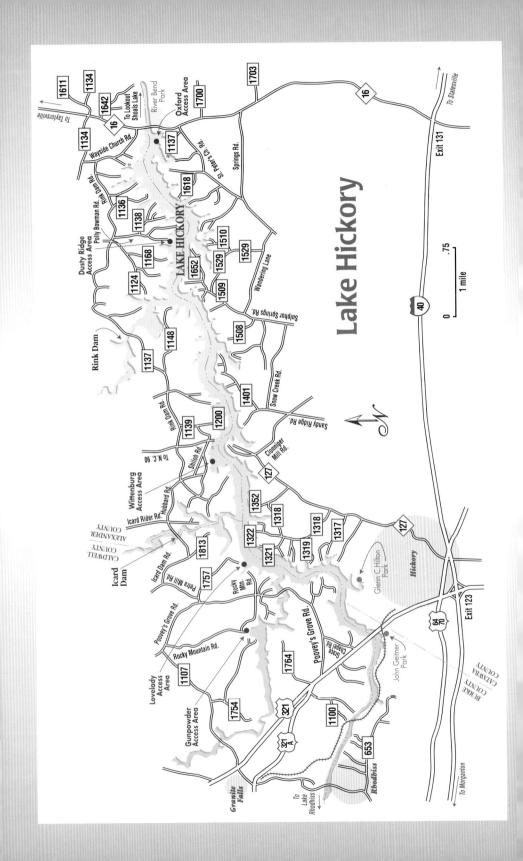

Lake Hickory

(continued from page 45)

rooms decorated with antiques. There is also a common parlor and business area. The grounds include gardens and birdfeeders. Information: 464 Seventh Street SW, Hickory, NC, (828) 324-0548 or (800) 654-2961.

Festivals and Events

Catawba Valley Pottery Festival – March: This festival showcases traditional pottery still made locally in the Catawba Valley. The history of pottery making in this area, with its German origins, is told through festival displays and exhibits. Potters offer their works for sale and give demonstrations of their craft. Information: (828) 322-3943.

Catawba Valley Storytelling Festival – May: Storytellers from throughout the Southeast bring their stories and stage shows to this festival every year in May. Hosted by the Catawba County Historical Association, the festival includes extensive programs for students of all ages and is held at the Murray's Mill historic site. Information: (828) 322-3943.

Riverfest at Catawba River Greenway – May: The City of Morganton hosts Riverfest the third Saturday in May at the Catawba River Greenway Park. Events center around canoeing the river and guided trips with free shuttle service are available. Running, rollerblading and skating are among the other activities of the day. Information: Recreation Department, (828) 438-5350.

Destinations: River Bend Park

Dedicated in 1999, this 450-acre park with one mile of river frontage in Newton, NC, is one of the largest non-state or federal parks in North Carolina. The park is also a notable success story for the Catawba River since it occupies land that was once designated for a landfill. When new environmental regulations made the prospect of a landfill too costly, county officials quickly realized that the tract would offer unparalleled recreational amenities to the citizens of Catawba County. Construction began in 1998 and, to stay under budget, county staff put in overtime and many volunteers hours contracting the work. Prison labor also allowed the park plans to include more than 12 miles of trail.

Location and hours: River Bend Park is in Newton, NC (see maps pages 48 and 50). From Asheville, follow Interstate 40 east to NC 16 (Exit 131). Turn left (north) onto NC 16 and follow about eight miles north to the well-marked park entrance.

The park is only open from Friday through Monday. From November through February, the hours are 8 a.m. to 6 p.m. In March and October, the hours are 8 a.m. to 7 p.m. and from April through September, it is open 8 a.m. to 8 p.m. The park is always closed Christmas Eve and Christmas Day.

There is no charge to enter the park or for activities including hiking, fishing or wildlife viewing. However, the park does require permits for

(continued to page 49)

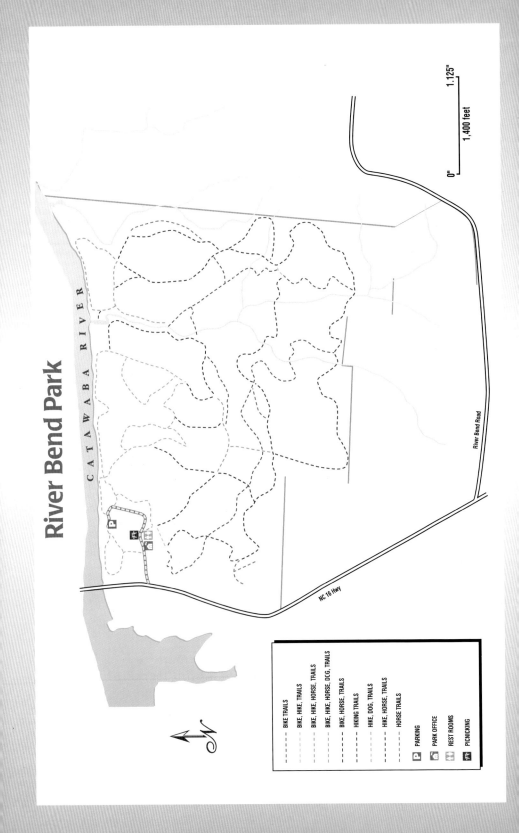

River Bend Park

CATAWABA RIVER

River Bend Road

NC 16 Hwy

N

0"   1,400 feet   1.125"

- - - - - BIKE TRAILS
- - - - - BIKE, HIKE, TRAILS
- - - - - BIKE, HIKE, HORSE, TRAILS
- - - - - BIKE, HIKE, HORSE, DCG, TRAILS
- - - - - BIKE, HORSE, TRAILS
- - - - - HIKING TRAILS
- - - - - HIKE, DOG, TRAILS
- - - - - HIKE, HORSE, TRAILS
- - - - - HORSE TRAILS

- P PARKING
- PARK OFFICE
- REST ROOMS
- PICNICKING

(continued from page 47)

grilling, boating, mountain biking and horseback riding. Fees range from $2.50 per day for paddling permits to $10 per day for a non-resident to mountain bike for the day. Contact the park for a complete fee schedule.

Things to do: River Bend Park offers almost unparalled resources for a county park with activities including fishing, picnicking, mountain biking, horseback riding and hiking. River Bend Park does not provide canoes or kayaks, but the park's access ramp will allow paddlers to put-in just below the Oxford Dam.

The trail network, in particular, will call to outdoor enthusiasts of all types. Mountain bikers can enjoy more than six miles of trail that include everything from technical single-track to fast, open multi-use trails. Be sure to stop off at the park office to obtain a biking permit.

All the trails at River Bend Park are open to hikers but some of the best used include a handicapped-accessible observation platform overlooking the Catawba River and flat, open trails beneath birches along the riverbanks. Since River Bend Park is located in a transitional area between the Piedmont and Appalachian foothills, the trails traverse a great diversity of ecosystems including several creeks, grassy meadows and a small pond. The higher hilltops within the park were once agricultural land that is now planted in three-decade old loblolly pine.

Wildlife viewing is popular at River Bend Park since the area is home to a variety of common Piedmont birds, reptiles and mammals. Bald eagles have been spotted on occasion.

The equestrian trails at River Bend Park begin from a large gravel parking lot above the park office where there is ample parking for horse trailers. The park requires valid proof of Coggins Test before visitors can obtain a horse-riding permit form the park office.

For more information: Contact River Bend Park at 6700 NC 16, North Conover, NC 28613, (828) 256-9157 or visit the county's web site (see appendix).

Destinations: Catawba Science Center

There is much more than science happening at this three-story building located right in the middle of Hickory's beautiful historic district. In fact the Science Center – which is an adaptive reuse of the old Claremont High School – is just part of the larger "SALT (Sciences-Art-Literature-Together) Block." The Science Center building also includes the renowned *(continued to page 51)*

PHOTO COURTESY PCF PRESS.

The Catawba Science Center is a popular attraction in Hickory, NC.

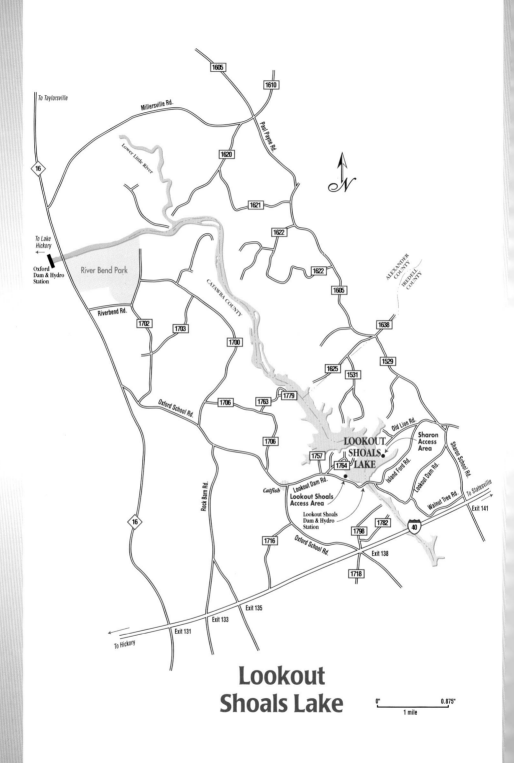

Lookout
Shoals Lake

0" 0.875"
1 mile

(continued from page 49)

Hickory Museum of Art, which is the second-oldest art museum in North Carolina. On the same block, you can also visit Patrick Beaver Memorial Library, which is the main facility for Hickory Public Libraries.

The Catawba Science Center includes a Naturalist Center, Physical Science Arcade and a Hall of Life Science. The center also hosts an array of traveling exhibits that rotate during the year. Across the hall at the Hickory Museum of Art, visitors can see more than 1,200 permanent pieces of art in four separate galleries as well as traveling exhibitions.

Location and hours: From Interstate 40, take Exit 125. From I-40 westbound, turn right off the exit ramp. From I-40 eastbound, turn left off the exit ramp. Travel 1.75 miles, though four lights and an underpass, then turn left. Travel one block and turn left at a light. Proceed 0.3 mile and bear to the right. The SALT Block is just ahead on the right.

The hours for Catawba Science Center and Hickory Museum of Art are similar. They are open Tuesday through Friday from 10 a.m. to 5 p.m. (the Museum of Art is open through 7:30 p.m. on Thursdays), 10 a.m. to 4 p.m. on Saturdays and 1 p.m. to 5 p.m. on Sundays, closed Mondays and major holidays.

Admission is $2 per person for adults, $1 for students and seniors. Children under 6 and members are free. The "Free Friday" program generally offers free admission each Friday.

What types of Traveling Exhibits come to the Museum of Art?

On a recent visit to the Hickory Museum of Art, the Coe Gallery was filled with blown glass, ceramics and paintings from the private collection of two Charlotte art collectors with a passion for North Carolina regional art. Since local artist Paul Whitener founded it in 1944, the Hickory Museum of Art has been a major artistic voice for the Catawba Valley. By focusing on contemporary American art, the museum has done a particularly good job of exposing and encouraging regional artists who specialize in landscapes, mountain photography and even Catawba Indian pottery. Check the web site for upcoming traveling exhibits (see appendix for web site).

What types of programs does the Catawba Science Center have for teachers and students?

The science center has many programs specifically for students K−12 as well as home school groups of between 10 and 30 students. The center will even take a traveling exhibition − the Rainforest Rescue Festival − out to schools in the Hickory area. The center's normal programs include physics presentations such as Newton's Amazement Park (eighth grade), earthquake simulators such as Quakes and Shakes (fourth grade) and even advanced programs such as biotechnology and "Pi Day." The Catawba Science Center makes its programs available to school groups during most normal operating hours, but since slots fill quickly teachers should call well in advance.

Science Center Exhibits-at-a-Glance:

Naturalist Center: Observe live reptiles, amphibians, insects and arachnids as well as preserved animals and fossils of many types.

PHOTO COURTESY PCF PRESS

The history of Bunker Hill Covered Bridge spans hundreds of years.

Hall of Life Science: Walk from the mountains to the sea in just a few feet! In this hallway, you can find out more about all the plants and animals of North Carolina in dynamic presentations such as "Mountain Stream."

KidSpace: A room full of science materials including magnifiers, a fish-eye view of Lake Hickory and a kid-sized generator.

Footprints Preschool Gallery: Explore a foam construction site, puppet theatre and other items for children under age 5.

Science Courtyard: Includes a simulated rock-climbing wall with a Piedmont tree house and sound experiments.

EarthWatch Center: Visitors can monitor current weather conditions, experience a simulated earthquake or volcanic eruption, and even experiment with clouds.

For more information: Call the Catawba Science Center at (828) 322-8169. Call the Hickory Museum of Art at (828) 327-8576. See appendix for web site information.

Day Trips: Bunker Hill Covered Bridge & Catawba County Museum of History

Most of us think about quaint New England towns when we see covered bridges. They evoke a more relaxed time of town meetings, political rallies and summertime fishing. In the Carolinas, the bridges are all but gone with rare exceptions: South Carolina has one and North Carolina two, including one on a tributary of the Catawba River.

The Bunker Hill Covered Bridge, built in 1894, allows passage over Lyle Creek in Catawba County, NC. Made of oak and wooden pins (instead of nails), the bridge spans 85 feet and was originally built as an open structure. It was covered with wooden shingles around 1899 and then re-covered with tin in 1921. A restoration in the mid-1990s stabilized the structure.

The bridge was recently named a National Civil Engineering Landmark, joining other North Carolina landmarks such as the Cape Hatteras Lighthouse and the Blue Ridge Parkway. Today, tucked away at the end of a short trail in a county park and bordered by a private hunting preserve, Bunker Hill Covered Bridge receives far less attention and is occasionally subject to vandalism and graffiti.

The history of this bridge and creek crossing spans hundreds of years. Bunker Hill Covered Bridge was initially part of Island Ford Road, a former Native American trail that became an important travel route in the development of Western North Carolina. During the Revolutionary War, the road offered a transportation route for British prisoners after the Battle of Cowpens in 1781.

More than a century later, in 1894, Catawba County commissioners asked local landowners to improve the crossing by building a bridge over Lyle Creek. Landowners hired the services of Andy L. Ramsour, keeper of the Horseford covered bridge over the Catawba River at Hickory. In 1895, Ramsour and several locals built the Bunker Hill Bridge. The bridge was named for a nearby farm operated by two local families.

The only other covered bridge in North Carolina is in Randolph County. South Carolina's covered bridge, Campbell Covered Bridge, is in Greenville County, north of Greer.

The Bunker Hill Covered Bridge and nearby Murray's Mill Museum Complex (a working flour mill and history complex which is open to the public) are two of the higher profile preservation projects of the Catawba County Historical Association. The association also maintains several family cemeteries in Catawba County and a popular museum in the county courthouse.

The three-story Catawba County Museum features permanent and traveling exhibits such as displays on Native American history and pottery, textile history and a major repository of Civil War artifacts.

BUNKER HILL COVERED BRIDGE

Directions: From Hickory, NC, follow US 70 east to the town of Claremont. Bunker Hill Covered Bridge is located two miles east of Claremont at the crossing of Lyle Creek (a tributary of the Catawba River).

Hours: Wednesday, Friday and Sunday 9 a.m. to 4 p.m.

CATAWBA COUNTY MUSEUM OF HISTORY

The Catawba County Museum of History is located on the court square in downtown Newton, NC. It is open Tuesday though Friday from 9 a.m. to 4 p.m. and Sunday from 2 to 5 p.m. Admission is free.

For more information: Call (828) 465-0383 for directions or details, or visit the Catawba County Historical Association online (see appendix).

PHOTO COURTESY CATAWBA COUNTY HISTORICAL ASSOCIATION.

The Catawba County Museum of History

Lake Norman in a quiet moment.

Lake Norman

If the size of a lake were the measure of its recreational potential, then Lake Norman would have to be regarded as the playground of the Catawba River. This massive body of water claims 32,475 acres of surface area and borders four counties stretching from Statesville to the northern reaches of Charlotte. Its 540 miles of shoreline accommodate one state park, three county parks, nine public boating accesses, two bank-fishing areas, fourteen marinas and too many private recreation facilities to mention — including golf courses and a college recreation campus. The lake even has its own magazine (*Lake Norman Magazine*), several web sites and smaller publications devoted to listing recreational opportunities!

Location

Lake Norman lies northwest of Charlotte, NC and is most easily accessed from Interstate 77, Exits 28 through 45.

Recreation: Paddling, Biking and Fishing

Lake Norman provides opportunities for almost every water-based recreational activity, from traditional pursuits to contemporary adventures such as parasailing and wakeboarding. There are numerous facilities where folks can also enjoy land-based activities such as hiking, biking, picnicking and camping.

Mecklenburg County operates the popular 106-acre **Jetton Park** on a peninsula off the southeastern shore of the lake. Jetton Park, which is close to Cornelius, includes a 1.5-mile walking trail as well as a 1.3-mile paved bicycle path that circles the park and connects amenities such as tennis courts, picnic decks and a waterfront hall for special events. The park is open daily from 8 a.m. to dusk and access costs $3 per vehicle if you are a resident of Mecklenburg County or $5 per vehicle if you are not a resident (fees apply only on weekends and holidays from March through October). Picnic sites at Jetton Park are available on a first-come, first-served basis. On weekends, bicycles can be rented in the Waterfront Plaza area for $4 an hour or $10 per day. Contact Jetton Park at 1900 Jetton Road, Cornelius, NC, (704) 896-9808. (See map page 58.)

Ramsey Creek Park in Cornelius, NC is a 46-acre park open from 7 a.m. to dark. Although less popular than Jetton Park, this area also features picnic areas, athletic fields and a nature trail. Call (704) 896-9808.

Near Huntersville, NC, the 26-acre **Blythe Landing County Park** also includes a picnic area, playground, four sand volleyball courts, walking trails and concessions. (See map page 58.)

While boating, water-skiing or fishing (not necessarily in that order) are probably the biggest reasons to visit Lake Norman, paddlers have some nice opportunities here as well. It is possible to launch canoes and kayaks from the boat ramp in **Lake Norman State Park** (see page 59) and, during the summer, rentals are available for use between 10 a.m. and 5:30 p.m. At **Wildlife Woods Campgrounds** (which is a full-service camp facility), visitors can also rent *(continued to page 57)*

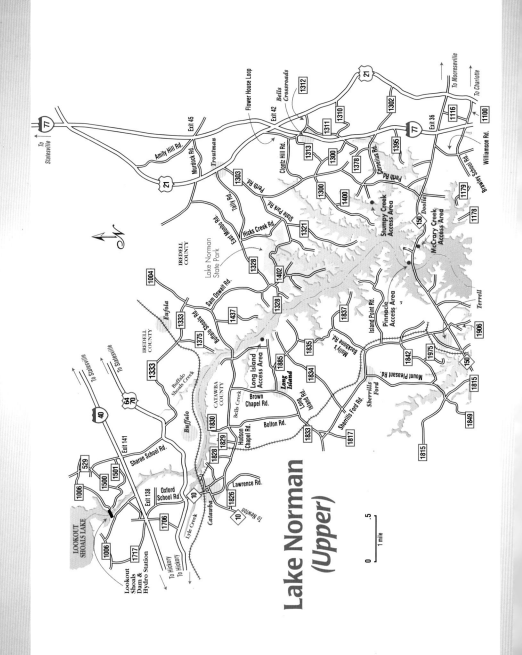

Lake Norman
(Upper)

0 ____ .5 ____ 1 mile

(continued from page 55)

canoes. Call (704) 483-5611 for more information. Check the Lake Norman map for public access areas.

Lake Norman offers an array of events for the diehard anglers among us, from annual big money tournaments to local Monday and Friday night bass-fishing competitions. If you're going out on your own, prepare to cast for a range of fish as the seasons change. Catfish, crappie, stripers and largemouth bass are exceptionally popular, especially during the yearly spawning in early spring. See the Fishing section (page 105) for more information about guide services. Fishing boat rentals are available in Troutman, NC at **Skipper's Dry Storage & Boat Rentals**. Rates run from $90 for a half day on a 17-foot fishing boat to $350 per day for a full day on a 21-foot deck boat. Call (704) 528-3328.

It is also possible to rent yachts, try parasailing or rent sailboats for the day at Lake Norman. Lake Norman Yacht Charters offers sailboats, a 67-foot houseboat and a 42-foot motor yacht. Call (704) 542-5492. Pontoon boats, sailboats and skiing boats are available from AAA-O Saltshaker Marine at (704) 892-5990. Parasailing is available through the North Harbor Marina. See the appendix for contact information and web sites.

Lakeside Camping and Nearby Bed & Breakfasts

There are numerous camping facilities, hotels, motels and other lodging opportunities near the Catawba River. This list primarily includes riverside camping opportunities or Bed & Breakfasts. These inns provide a comfortable alternative to camping, and allow visitors to expe-rience the sights and recreation of the river in a multi-day experience.

Cross Country Campgrounds: 400 sites, full service and tent sites. 3 bathhouses, fishing lake, nature trails, playground, basketball and shuffleboard courts. Information: 6254 Hwy 150 E., Denver, NC, (704) 483-5897.

Wildlife Woods Campgrounds: 200 sites on Lake Norman with full service and tent sites available. Pool, boat dock, game room, recreation hall, paddleboat and canoe rentals. Information: 10.5 miles west of I-77 on NC 150, Denver, NC, (704) 483-5611.

Lake Norman State Park: 33 tent and trailer sites with tent pads, picnic tables, fire rings and grills. Water and restrooms available nearby. Information: (see below for more details) Exit 42 off I-77 on Lake Norman.

Tower House Bed and Breakfast: This inn was built in 1903 and is located in the historic district of Statesville, NC. There are three guest rooms with private baths and two common parlors. The inn is within walking distance to downtown shops and restaurants. Information: 530 W. Front Street, Statesville, NC, (704) 883-0328 or (800) 844-1883.

Festivals and Events

Highland Games – April: Deeply rooted in legend and folklore, these Scottish games mimic the organized competitions of soldiers and runners started nearly 2000 years ago. The festival celebrates the heritage of many of the settlers in this area of North Carolina and offers cultural entertainment through this

(continued to page 59)

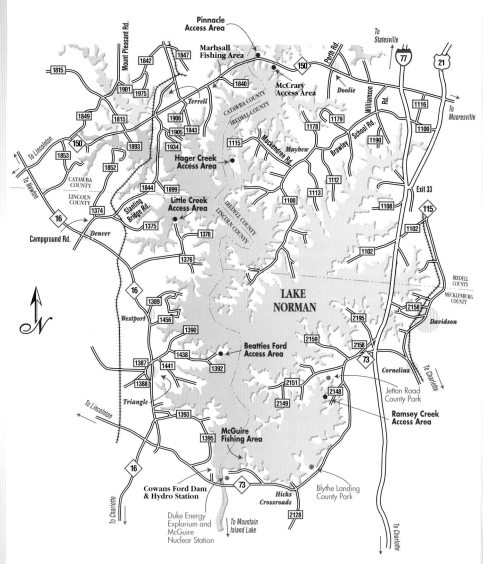

Lake Norman
(Lower)

0   .5

1 mile

(continued from page 57)

multi-day event. For information, contact the Catawba Valley Scottish Society at (704) 875-3113 or visit the society's web site for more information (see appendix.)

National Balloon Rally – September: One of the oldest balloon rallies in the world comes to Statesville, NC each September. Most years, balloons and skydivers help kick off the festival with the mass lift-off of between 50 and 75 balloons. Call (704) 873-2892.

Destinations: Lake Norman State Park
(formerly Duke Power State Park)

Situated on the northeastern shore of Lake Norman, this park sprawls for 1,362 gorgeous acres with its own 33-acre lake where visitors can rent pedal boats, rowboats and canoes. There are 33 tent and trailer camping sites, and two picnic areas in the park with tables and grills. Hikers can enjoy a short stroll or a long trek on trails that range from just under a mile to almost seven miles in length. Ramp access to Lake Norman is available, as well as a swimming beach – the only one on Lake Norman.

Location and hours: Take Exit 42 off Interstate 77 in Iredell County and follow signs to the park entrance. Lake Norman State Park opens daily at 8 a.m. year-round, and the park office hours are Monday to Friday from 8 a.m. to 5 p.m. (See maps on pages 56 and 60.)

The North Carolina Division of Parks and Recreation does not charge entrance fees for its parks.

Costs in the parks are associated with use of certain facilities such as boat rentals, camping, swimming and cabins. Fees range from $3 to rent a canoe, $8 for primitive campsites and $20 for picnic shelter reservations.

Things to do: From group tent camping to daylong hikes, Lake Norman State Park has long been a mecca for visitors seeking passive recreation opportunities on the shores of North Carolina's largest lake. The park is also home to the only public swimming area on the entire lake. In recent years, mountain bikers and park officials have begun building some exciting new trails. These trails are currently in the preliminary stages, but will be open to the public soon.

An easy 0.8-mile loop trail (the Alder Trail) crosses the picnic area and follows the shoreline, while a moderate 6.7-mile trail (the Lakeshore Trail) loops around the peninsula and passes the campground. Spur trails and cutoffs showcase the other areas of the park. Both the Alder Trail and the Lakeshore Trail dart in and out of a forest of hickory, pine, poplar and oak; neither gains more than 50 feet of overall elevation.

Ecologically, Lake Norman State Park is a mix of pine and hardwood forests that have been hit hard by natural phenomena in recent years. In 1989, Hurricane Hugo downed thousands of trees, especially on the park's higher eastern ridges. More recently, an infestation of Southern Pine Beetles has reduced the pines to small pockets surrounded by a predominantly hardwood forest.

For more information: Contact Lake Norman State Park, 159 Inland Sea Lane, Troutman, NC 28166. Call (704) 528-6350. Visit the North

(continued to page 61)

Lake Norman State Park

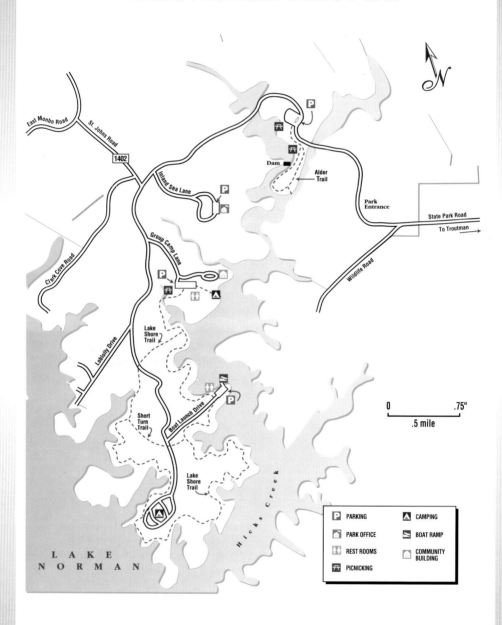

(continued from page 59)

Carolina Division of Parks and Recreation web site (see appendix) for details.

Destinations: Duke Visitor Centers

Duke Energy offers two Nuclear Station visitor centers along the Catawba River corridor. The largest center, the Energy Explorium, is located on Lake Norman as part of the McGuire Nuclear Station complex. This center offers displays and exhibits that educate visitors on the energy generation and environmental management practices of the site.

There are numerous interactive programs and presentations available to visitors inside the center. Outside, various displays, plaques and markers provide information along the landscaped shores of Lake Norman. A nature trail winds through the woods along the lake and offers wildlife exhibits.

The second visitor center, Energy Quest, is located on Lake Wylie at the Catawba Nuclear Station. Much as the Energy Explorium, this center offers a self-guided, interactive tour and includes displays, exhibits and a theater. A short nature trail and an amphitheater are located outside the center on the shores of Lake Wylie.

Location and hours: For the Energy Explorium, take Exit 28 off Interstate 77 and follow NC 73 west toward Lake Norman. The complex will be on the right. For Energy Quest, take Exit 82B off Interstate 77 and follow SC 161 west to SC 274 north. Turn right onto Concord Road. The complex is on the left. (See map page 82.)

The Energy Explorium is open Monday to Friday from 9 a.m. to 5 p.m., from noon to 5 p.m. on Saturday and Sunday. Energy Quest is open Monday through Friday from 9 a.m. to 5 p.m. by appointment only. Call (800) 777-0006.

The Energy Explorium: If you have ever wondered how energy is produced and how it all relates to the hydroelectric and nuclear stations along the Catawba, this visitor center near the dam at Lake Norman can provide the answers.

As visitors walk through the hall of exhibits, they are presented with an array of entertaining and educational displays, tours and programs. The interactive desk "Operator For a Day" allows a guest to experience "powering up" McGuire Nuclear Station. A nearby video center offers a virtual tour of McGuire, and explains how energy is produced. Visual displays and information fact sheets outline Duke Energy's commitment to environmental management.

The visitor center is especially child-friendly. Megawatt, the energy dog, is the central character of an interactive video program designed to teach children ways to save energy. Help Megawatt find all his bones by identifying objects that can waste energy. Another video program features Ollie the bird, who explains his environment and how to care for it.

Other exhibits include a fossil fuel and hydroelectric power display. A weather tracker offers satellite views, current temperatures, local weather, wind speeds and lake surface water temperatures.

Things to do: The visitor center at McGuire Nuclear Station offers boardwalks and picnic facilities for

The Catawba Queen (left and Catawba Belle (right) are replicas of famous Mississippi paddle wheelers.

guests to enjoy the view of Lake Norman and its natural areas. Among the informative wildlife plaques is a description of special programs for Osprey habitats. Duke Energy has given these raptors special attention by providing for nesting sites near the station. Ospreys are large fish-eating birds found along lakes and waterways. Their nests are huge structures sometimes measuring three feet deep by three feet wide. They prefer tops of dead trees, poles or channel markers, and return to the same nest year after year. Another beneficiary of Duke's environmental program is the Eastern Bluebird. The many houses built on or near transmission towers create "bluebird trails" throughout the company's service area.

A mile-long trail leaves the visitor center and takes hikers on a winding trip through the forest along the lake's shores. A fish-friendly pier and backyard wildlife habitat are examples of the environments created to foster wildlife. The exhibits along the trail include a reptile and amphibian pond, and osprey platforms.

For more information: Contact the Energy Explorium at (800) 777-0003 or (704) 875-5600 or visit the company's web site for more information (see appendix). For Energy Quest, call (800) 777-0006 or (803) 831-3609.

Day Trips: Catawba Cruises

One of the lesser known but increasingly popular trips open for Catawba River visitors are lake tours and dinner cruises.

On Lake James, the "Harbor Queen," a 38-foot pontoon boat with roof, has been operating since 1988, said owner Reid Scott. On Lake Norman, the first tours began in 1991 when Charlotte-area businessmen Bud Lancaster and Jack Williams decided to launch the "Catawba Queen."

A replica of the famous Mississippi River paddle wheelers,

the Catawba Queen was built in Wisconsin, then cruised down the Mississippi to the Gulf of Mexico before steaming over to Miami. The boat continued up the Atlantic Coast to Wilmington where it was disassembled and transported to Lake Norman for service.

On a recent visit, Williams delighted in showing visitors around the premises. Queens Landing, the marina that serves both boats and has many slips for other visitors, also includes a carpeted golf course and lakeside deli. For several years, the Catawba Queen did all of the sightseeing and dinner cruises on the lake until demand became so great that the Queens Landing owners decided to invest in an additional boat, the "Catawba Belle."

Now, both boats operate side-by-side and stay busy almost 'round the clock during the peak season of April through September. The Queen is a plush ferryboat with covered top deck and spacious main deck that offers comfort even in inclement weather. The menu does change occasionally, but on a recent trip we had a choice of prime rib or steamed shrimp. The meals include salad, baked potato and cheesecake for dessert. While the tours are enjoyable any time of the year, they are certainly best during summer weather.

On Lake James, accommodations are a little more Spartan. The Harbor Queen runs out of Mountain Harbor Marina, primarily during the peak months of May through September. Scott, who owns the boat and marina, said it's hard to gauge how many tours the Queen makes, but they generally do not go out in bad weather.

If you choose to take the Harbor Queen, you'll have two options:

touring the western portion of the Catawba River or venturing further up onto Lake James. Scott says its hard to decide which trip is best — the Catawba River tour often includes bald eagle sightings but the Lake James tour includes excellent views of Shortoff Mountain and Graveyard Island.

Lake Norman: QUEENS LANDING

Tours: The Catawba Queen and Catawba Belle regularly run luncheon, sightseeing and dinner cruises. Chartered trips and specialty cruises are available. Dinner cruises generally run between 2 and 2.5 hours.

Sightseeing & Luncheon Cruises: (call ahead for menu and boarding times) October 1 through March 31 — all cruises by reservation only; April 1 through April 30 — Monday through Friday; May 1 through Sept. 30 — open 7 days.

Costs: Sightseeing ($7 for children to $11 for adults); luncheon ($13 for children to $18 for adults); dinner cruises run year-round, although you'll need to call ahead for boarding times, menu and to make reservations ($32 for children to $48 for adults).

For more information: Call Queens Landing at (704) 663-2628 or visit Queen's Landing online (see appendix).

Lake James: THE HARBOR QUEEN AT MOUNTAIN HARBOR MARINA

Tours: 2.5 to 3 hours. Bring your own picnic. The boat generally does not go out in bad weather.

Costs: $10 per person with a minimum of eight people per trip.

For more information: Call Mountain Harbor Marina at (828) 584-0666.

Mountain Island Lake is home to wildlife refuges and nature preserves.

Mountain Island Lake

South of Lake Norman, the Catawba River flows back and forth through elbow turns before the Mountain Island Dam holds it in an S-shaped lake. In many ways, Mountain Island Lake stands in stark contrast to Lake Norman. To begin with, 3,281 acres of surface area and 61 miles of shoreline make this lake one-tenth the size of its Catawba neighbor to the north. More notably, while Lake Norman's shores are lined with permanent and weekend homes and some golf courses, the shores of Mountain Island Lake are mostly home to wildlife refuges and nature preserves. Two public access points offer boating and water sports to residents and visitors of Mountain Island Lake. Residents and visitors, however, are more likely to be eagles, ducks, osprey and herons rather than humans. As with all the lakes of the Catawba, Mountain Island Lake offers a variety of outdoor recreation opportunities.

Location

Mountain Island Lake separates Mecklenburg and Gaston counties in North Carolina. NC 16 travels across the lake and along the west side while NC 27 and Beatties Ford Road follow the east side.

Recreation: Paddling, Biking and Fishing

Boating, fishing and swimming are popular lake activities; however, Mountain Island Lake also offers an impressive variety of land-based recreation. Hiking, biking, camping, nature observation and equestrian

opportunities are found in the lakeside refuges and preserves. History plays a role at Latta Plantation and Rural Hill Nature preserves, both along the lake's eastern shores. Wildlife education takes a unique twist at the **Carolina Raptor Center,** also located here. Mountain Island Lake's combination of water and land activities offers something for everyone.

Cowans Ford Wildlife Refuge, a limited access area, encompasses 901 acres inside a horseshoe bend of Mountain Island Lake (see map page 66). It is operated by Mecklenburg County Parks and Recreation, and offers an observation deck for wildlife viewing. The quiet coves and inland lakes of the refuge attract a large wading bird population as well as many other species of waterfowl. The preserve offers scheduled educational programs and classes. To reach Cowans Ford Wildlife

(continued to page 67)

PHOTO COURTESY OF MECKLENBURG COUNTY.

Examining salamander eggs with students at the Cowans Ford Wildlife Refuge, a limited access area operated by Mecklenburg County Parks & Recreation.

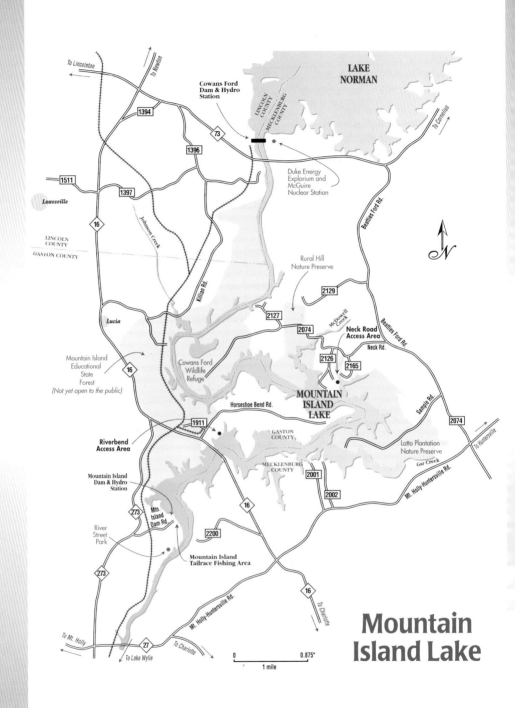

Mountain Island Lake

To Lincolnton
To Newton
LAKE NORMAN
Cowans Ford Dam & Hydro Station
1394
73
1396
To Cornelius
LINCOLN COUNTY
MECKLENBURG COUNTY
1511
1397
Lowesville
Duke Energy Explorium and McGuire Nuclear Station
Johnson Creek
16
LINCOLN COUNTY
GASTON COUNTY
Rural Hill Nature Preserve
Beatties Ford Rd.
2129
Killian Rd.
2127
Lucia
2074
McDowell Creek
Neck Road Access Area
Beatties Ford Rd.
Neck Rd.
Mountain Island Educational State Forest (Not yet open to the public)
16
Cowans Ford Wildlife Refuge
2126
2165
MOUNTAIN ISLAND LAKE
Sample Rd.
2074
To Huntersville
Horseshoe Bend Rd.
1911
GASTON COUNTY
MECKLENBURG COUNTY
Latta Plantation Nature Preserve
Gar Creek
Riverbend Access Area
2001
Mountain Island Dam & Hydro Station
273
Mtn. Island Dam Rd.
16
2002
Mt. Holly-Huntersville Rd.
River Street Park
2200
Mountain Island Tailrace Fishing Area
273
16
To Charlotte
To Mt. Holly
27
Mt. Holly-Huntersville Rd.
To Charlotte
To Lake Wylie

0   0.875"
1 mile

(continued from page 65)

Refuge, follow Beatties Ford Road to Neck Road. Follow Neck Road to a dirt road on the left. There is a parking area at the end. Contact the Mecklenburg County Parks and Recreation Department for more information (see appendix for web site).

Rural Hill Nature Preserve, which is just a short distance downstream from Cowans Ford, does not feature any public facilities. But ownership of the site by Mecklenburg County Parks and Recreation ensures protection of the 265-acre site and its natural resources. Major John Davidson, a prominent figure in Mecklenburg County who served in the Revolutionary War, built Rural Hill Plantation in 1788. As one of the finest Catawba River plantations, the site had more than 5,000 acres and many structures including the grand mansion home with a detached 2-story kitchen, a smokehouse, well house, crib, grainery and two schoolhouses. While there are some ruins and evidence of the original buildings, the detached kitchen house still exists today and is the office of the Catawba Valley Scottish Society. Rural Hill Nature Preserve is located on Neck Road in Mecklenburg County just before Cowans Ford Wildlife Refuge. Visit the county's web page (see appendix) for more information.

In the coming years, visitors to the **Mountain Island Educational State Forest** will have an extraordinary number of recreational and educational amenities at their fingertips. This new forest (established in 2000) straddles the county line between Lincoln and Gaston counties. The North Carolina Division of Forest Resources is busy with road reclamation projects and transforming unused cutovers into a wildlife demonstration area. As of summer 2002, the forest was closed to the public, but is open to schools and educational groups for ranger-led classes and events. Contact the forest at 1933 Mountain Island Highway, Mount Holly, NC. Call (704) 827-7576 or visit the agency's web page for more information (see appendix).

In July 2002, the city of Mount Holly opened the first public park along the Catawba River in Gaston County below Mountain Island Dam. The 46-acre site includes a one-mile trail and an adjoining fishing pier maintained by the NC Wildlife Commission. Mount Holly has big plans for the area in the future, including a boat launch, picnic tables and primitive campsites. The park is located at the northernmost portion of Lake Wylie and below the dam. From Mount Holly, drive north on NC 273 about a half-mile down Mountain Island Road.

Lakeside Camping and Nearby Bed & Breakfasts

There are numerous camping facilities, hotels, motels and other lodging opportunities near the Catawba River. This list primarily includes riverside camping opportunities or Bed & Breakfasts. These inns provide a comfortable alternative to camping, and allow visitors to experience the sights and recreation of the river in a multi-day experience.

There is no riverside camping in the Mountain Island Lake vicinity.

Robin's Nest Bed and Breakfast:
This 1914 Classical Revival inn is located in Mt. Holly between Mountain Island Lake and Lake Wylie. Four guest rooms with
(continued to page 69)

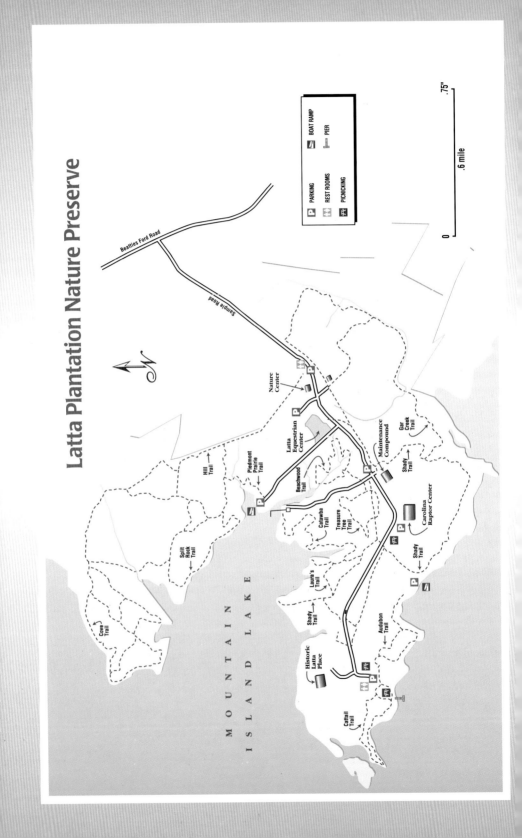

Latta Plantation Nature Preserve

(continued from page 67)

private baths are named after the birds you are likely to see on the grounds. There are also two sitting rooms for guests to enjoy. Information: 156 N. Main Street, Mt. Holly, NC, (704) 827-2420 or (888) 711-NEST.

Destinations: Latta Plantation Nature Preserve

Latta Plantation Nature Preserve occupies more than 1,290 acres on the eastern shores of Mountain Island Lake in Mecklenburg County, NC, and provides Charlotte residents with the county's largest nature preserve. This preserve offers the perfect opportunity for outdoor enthusiasts to enjoy water-based and land-based recreation in one location. The park includes an extensive hiking and horseback riding trail system (more than 16 miles), picnic shelters with tables and grills, canoe access to Mountain Island Lake with boat rentals and plenty of fishing opportunities. Other facilities in the park include an equestrian center, nature center (which serves as the gateway to the entire preserve), the Historic Latta Plantation and the Carolina Raptor Center.

Location and hours: From Interstate 77, take Exit 16-B (Sunset Road West). Turn right at the second light onto Beatties Ford Road. Go approximately 5 miles. Turn left onto Sample Road. (See maps on pages 66 and 68.)

Latta Plantation Nature Preserve is open daily from 7 a.m. to sunset. There are no fees to enter the nature preserve or to use the nature center. (The nature center is open Monday through Saturday from 9 a.m. to 5 p.m. and Sunday 1 p.m. to 5 p.m.) The equestrian center is open Monday through Friday from 10 a.m. to 3 p.m. and on weekends from 10 a.m. to 5 p.m. Trail rides are $18 per person (ages 8 and up) and $4 for pony rides.

Historic Latta Plantation is open Tuesday through Friday from 10 a.m. to 5 p.m. and weekends from noon to 5 p.m. The entrance fee is $4 for adults, $3 for students and seniors, and $2 for children ages 7 to 12.

Things to do: The Latta Plantation Nature Center houses an impressive collection of exhibits and educational materials. There are many displays, including some live animals, which showcase the variety of flora and fauna found in the preserve. Maps and photos tell of on-site projects such as a Piedmont Prairie restoration, which protects the federally endangered Schweinitz's Sunflower. There is also a gift shop and information on the facilities throughout the park.

An overlook at Latta Plantation, which is Mecklenburg County's largest nature preserve.

The 1,290-acre preserve also includes 17 different trails ranging in length from 0.3 miles to 1.4 miles. The trails are looped to allow for longer hikes and the entire system includes more than 18 miles. There are no designated bike trails in Latta Plantation but the roads and paved areas throughout the park are open to bicycle use.

Conversely, the Equestrian Center makes full use of the preserve trails. Parking and unloading areas are available for guests bringing their own horses and the center also offers guided trail rides from the larger stables (by appointment). The center offers local residents western and English riding programs and day camps as well as a professional show operation.

Historic Latta Plantation is part of a 100-acre plot of land along the Catawba River purchased by James Latta in 1799. The following year, he built a two-story Federal-style house, which was quite unique in the area at that time. Over the next 20 years, Latta became a large plantation owner, having accumulated an additional 600 acres and numerous slaves. Cotton was the primary crop; however, crops and livestock needed to support the plantation were also raised on-site. Latta died in 1837 and, in the century following, the property changed ownership several times. In 1922, the property was sold to the Catawba Power Company. The house and much of the property remained after the development of Mountain Island Lake, so Duke Power donated the structure to Latta Place, a non-profit organization that still runs the museum today. In 1975, the additional acreage that makes up Latta Plantation Nature Preserve was purchased by Mecklenburg County. Today, the house is completely restored and furnished according to Latta's time period. Visitors can tour the home, its outbuildings and the surrounding 52-acre living history farm. Scheduled tours run from the museum center. The historic plantation also holds annual festivals and events.

For more information: Latta Plantation Nature Preserve is located at 5226 Sample Road in Mecklenburg County, NC. Call (704) 875-1931 or visit the Mecklenburg County Parks and Recreation Department web site online (see appendix).

Destinations: Carolina Raptor Center

This environmental education, rehabilitation and research center is dedicated to the care and protection of orphaned and injured birds of prey. The center receives hundreds of raptors from all over the region. The birds are rehabilitated at the medical facility and released back into the wild. Those unable to be released reside at the site and can be observed and enjoyed by visitors.

The center occupies 57 acres inside Latta Plantation Nature Preserve on Mountain Island Lake and includes an environmental education center offering exhibits and programs, and a gift shop with a large selection of souvenirs and educational items. Outdoors, the focal point of the center is an interpretive trail with kiosks and aviaries, which enthrall visitors by offering close encounters with many species of raptors.

Location and hours: From Interstate 77, take Exit 16-B (Sunset Road West). Turn right at the second light onto Beatties Ford Road. Travel approximately five miles. Turn left onto Sample Road and enter Latta Plantation Nature Preserve. Travel 0.6 mile to Carolina Raptor Center on the left. (See maps pages 66 and 68.)

The Carolina Raptor Center is open Tuesday to Saturday from 10 a.m. to 5 p.m. and from noon to 5 p.m. on Sunday.

Admission is $5 per person for adults, students and senior citizens are $3, children under 6 and members are free.

What are Raptors? Raptors are known as birds of prey and include eagles, owls, hawks and falcons. These birds are often magnificent in size and stature, and spotting them in the wild is a special experience for even the most seasoned bird watchers. Raptors feed on mice, rats, snakes and other small animals, and use their sharp talons to catch and kill their prey. They are considered to be at the top of the food chain, which makes their population an indicator of our environment's health.

The Interpretive Trail: The trail at Carolina Raptor Center gives visitors a chance to appreciate raptors in an up-close and safe environment. As you leave the main building and gift shop, the trail breaks into a series of loops. An open display area hosts interpretive programs. Numbered aviaries with kiosks dot the trail, which is appropriately mapped. Among the birds you can expect to find are a variety of hawks and

Coopers. Owls such as the eastern screech and great horned stare piercingly as you pass. Peregrine falcons and Mississippi kites perch on limbs and majestic red-tailed hawks show off their plumage. The largest display is home to numerous bald and golden eagles who proudly captivate their visitor's attention.

Most of the displays include educational information, and sometimes the specific injuries and histories of the birds. The trail is about one mile in length and returns to the education center.

The Education Building: This 4,000-square-foot complex houses the medical and research facilities for the Raptor Center. Hundreds of birds are brought to the center each year with illness or injuries. Some birds have survived gunshot wounds and amputations. According to the center, one of the most common injury causes for such birds is being hit by a car, usually the result of roadside littering.

(continued to page 73)

The Carolina Raptor Center provides care and protection for raptors such as this kestrel.

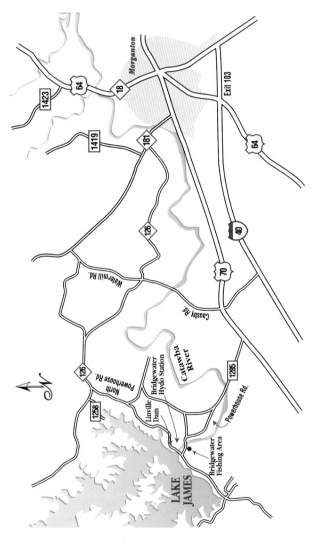

Free Flowing Catawba
From Bridgewater to Catawba River Greenway

0   0.625"
|———————|
1 mile

(continued from page 71)

The building also has an exhibit area where many educational displays and materials are offered. The center's staff and volunteers offer educational programs on-site as well as for schools and organizations throughout the Southeast.

For more information: The Carolina Raptor Center is a non-profit and member organization. Call: 704-875-6521 or visit the center's web site (see appendix).

Day Trips: Paddling the Free-Flowing Catawba

Paddling the Catawba River means something different to almost everyone who has ever done it.

In North Carolina it sometimes involves exploring the open waters of Lake Norman or, if you're inclined to adventure, perhaps doing the one-day float between Lake James and Morganton.

In South Carolina — where it's possible to find one of the longest free-flowing sections on the river — paddling the Catawba means picking your way through shoals and the kind of small drops that barely tease moderately skilled boaters. It's not hard to find a day's worth of solitude here, although those of you inclined to the hairball side of paddling will want to search elsewhere.

But for what the Catawba River lacks in glamour and heart-stopping excitement, it more than makes up in overall adventure quotient.

If one were to consider tackling the entire corridor, it would involve an expedition mentality and a willingness to deal with storms, exhausting portages, wilderness camping and confusing directions. Few paddlers in the Carolinas can claim to have actually paddled the entire river from mountains to Lake Wateree. Mike Fischesser is one.

Over a seven-month stretch in 1997-98, Fischesser led a crew of students from his Morganton, N.C.-based outdoor program on a canoe trip across the Carolinas to raise money for Habitat for Humanity. The 400-mile trip (the crew eventually finished by paddling into the Atlantic) netted more than $3,000 for the charity and helped the team prepare for a major expedition in Canada's Northwest Territories.

Rather than attempt the entire Catawba in one shot, the teams broke their float into a series of stages. On their initial forays west of Old Fort, the students learned the basics of flat water paddling and first experienced all the joys of canoe tours… torn dry-bags, sand-covered clothes, ruined maps.

The following stretches involved casual paddles across Lake James as well as spirit-sapping portages around hydro stations on Lake Hickory and, shortly afterward, Lookout Shoals. Fischesser said the teams did not plan campsites in advance, preferring to wing it in search of wilderness sites or — on occasion — even paddling through the night.

"The magic of the whole expedition was that we were going to the ocean," Fischesser said. "Even compared to paddling through the Arctic Circle, the Catawba just really had an element of adventure — an

(continued to page 75)

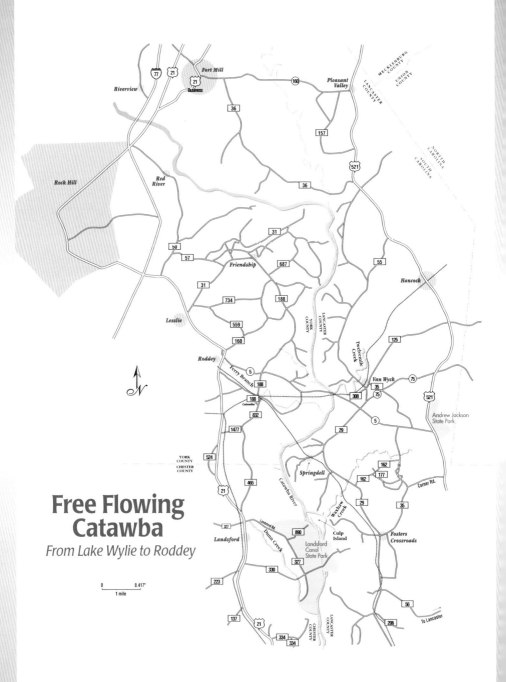

Free Flowing
Catawba
From Lake Wylie to Roddey

(continued from page 73)
element of the unknown – that you can't understand unless you go out and try it."

And in truth it's hard to understand Fischesser's charm until you have paddled the river. Because the free-flowing sections of the Catawba – especially those in South Carolina – pass through such remote country, many first time visitors prefer short day trips.

In North Carolina, one excellent free-flowing section of the Catawba begins in the shadow of Linville Dam. For a mile after the put-in at Bridgewater Fishing Area the Catawba is big water, rushing in fits of gorgeous blue-green and – depending on the water release schedule from the dam – perhaps best paddled with some experience under your belt. Shortly, the Catawba reaches a confluence with the aptly named Muddy Creek and begins a

languid stroll east, requiring only one easy portage near the trip's end.

This paddle is probably best incorporated into a fishing trip. There are several points along the way where the fishing is excellent and the river passes numerous bluffs, rope swings and sandy banks fit for lunch. The take out for this section is the Catawba River Greenway in Morganton.

One of the best sections on the entire river is the 31-mile stretch in South Carolina between the Lake Wylie dam to the S.C. 9 bridge near Lancaster. Beginning just below the dam, the river is surrounded by a variety of forest types and open treeless areas. The animal life in this area is among the most diverse in all of South Carolina. It is common to watch bald eagles, osprey, and red-shouldered hawks during the day while listening to great horned owls at night. Great egret, great blue

The Catawba River offers enjoyable paddling on free-flowing sections in both North and South Carolina.

Paddlers listen for tips before putting in at Landsford Canal. Many people paddle a seven-mile trail on the Catawba River that begins here.

herons wade through the water and – in early spring – songbirds fill the surrounding environment.

If you choose to put in at Landsford Canal State Park (a popular 7.4-mile day float begins here), you will not actually put in to the main current of the river. An island (which actually looks like the far shore) sits smack dab in the middle of the Catawba and you'll have to paddle a short distance upstream and around the huge island to reach the main channel. When you reach the south end of the island, aim river-left for the best flow through the shoals. In drought years, the flow can be difficult to navigate and may require some ingenuity. The paddling in the Fishing Creek and Cedar Creek Reservoir area is also extremely popular. See page 91 for details.

Paddling THE FREE-FLOWING CATAWBA IN NORTH CAROLINA

Put-in: Bridgewater Fishing Area (see page 36 for a map of Lake James or page 72 for section map)

Take-out: Catawba River Greenway in Morganton

Length: Approximately 10 miles (5+ hours depending on water flow)

Difficulty level: easy (One mandatory portage above Catawba Greenway.)

Directions: *For Bridgewater Fishing Area*, from Morganton, follow US 70 west approximately nine miles to North Powerhouse Road (SR-1223). Turn right and follow to Bridgewater Fishing Area access.

For Catawba River Greenway, from Morganton, follow US 70 (West Union Drive) east to the junction with US 70 Business (Fleming Drive) and US 64 (Sanford Drive). Continue east for 0.5 miles to Greenlee Ford Road on the right. Follow Greenlee Ford 0.25-mile to the greenway entrance. The Greenway can also be accessed through a boardwalk adjoining J. Barton's Restaurant off Sanford Drive.

For more information: Call Duke Power for Lake James levels and release information, (800) 829-5253 or visit the power company's web page (see appendix).

Paddling THE FREE-FLOWING CATAWBA IN SOUTH CAROLINA

Put-in: Fort Mill Access Area just downstream of the Lake Wylie dam (see page 82 for a map of (lower) Lake Wylie)

Take-out: SC 9 Bridge (see page 94 for a map of Fishing Creek Reservoir or page 74 for section map)

Length: 31 miles (Most paddlers do this as a two-day trip but remember, there is no camping at Landsford Canal State Park).

Difficulty level: easy

Runnable levels & additional notes: If the release from Lake Wylie is around 80 cubic feet per minute, the water may be too low. Release levels also get as high as 11,800 cubic feet per minute, making normally Class I rapids into Class II or III. It is also possible to break this float into as many as four separate, shorter trips. One popular version is a 7.4-mile trip that begins at Landsford Canal State Park and ends at the SC 9 Bridge landing. Another popular day trip begins at the Fort Mill Access Area and runs down to River Park in Rock Hill. This five-mile

section follows a wonderful section of the river.

Directions: *For Fort Mill Access Area,* from Exit 83 on Interstate 77. Follow SC 49 north to a left turn onto SC 251. The access area is at the end of this road.

For Landsford Canal State Park, from Exit 65 on Interstate 77 near Chester, drive east on SC 9 for 1.2 miles and turn left onto SC 223. When SC 223 ends at US 21, turn left and then right onto Chester County S-12330. Drive 2.2 miles and turn left onto S-12327. Drive 1.3 miles and turn right into the park. The put-in is at the bottom of the hill at a picnic area with bathrooms and a kiosk.

For SC 9 Landing, from Landsford Canal State Park, turn left onto S-12327. Drive 1.3 miles and turn right onto S-12330. Drive 2.2 miles and turn left onto US 21. Drive 5.5 miles and turn left onto SC 9. Drive 1.7 miles, cross over the bridge and the landing is on the left.

Copperhead Island, which is located on Lake
Wylie just across from McDowell Nature Preserve.

Lake Wylie

Lake Wylie marks the Catawba River's journey from North Carolina into South Carolina with the main body of the lake serving as the boundary between the two states. Lake Wylie was originally called Catawba Lake and is the oldest lake along the river corridor. It has a surface area of 13,443 acres and 325 miles of shoreline. Numerous creeks and tributaries, including the South Fork of the Catawba River flowing south from its origin in Catawba County, NC, contribute to the lake's spine-like corridor. As are the other lakes in the Catawba system, Lake Wylie is a playground for outdoor enthusiasts and hosts notable attractions such as McDowell Nature Preserve and Daniel Stowe Botanical Gardens. If you plan to fish on Lake Wylie, keep in mind that you may need to be licensed in both North and South Carolina.

Location

Lake Wylie lies southwest of Charlotte, NC. Interstate 85 crosses north of the main body of the lake and Interstate 77 parallels the eastern shoreline.

Recreation: Paddling, Biking and Fishing

As the third largest lake on the Catawba, Lake Wylie has much to offer for the outdoor enthusiast. Public boat launches, canoe put-ins and fishing areas dot the shoreline along with numerous marinas. Land-based recreation opportunities can be found at lakeside parks and preserves while the lesser-known spots including the **Catawba Riverfront Mountain Bike Park** and nearby **Anne Springs Close Greenway** offers hiking, mountain biking, equestrian trails and environmental education programs.

At the Catawba Riverfront Mountain Bike Park, Charlotte area riders have put plenty of work into the 8.5-mile loop trail. A "rooty" trail with some steep downhills and tough climbs, this trail is a regional favorite since it ambles along the river and is easily accessible (even visible!) from Interstate 85. To find the trail from Charlotte, drive south on I-85 to Sam Wilson Road (Exit 29). Take an immediate left onto Performance Road and follow until it ends at Moores Chapel Road. Turn left onto Moores Chapel Road and then make your first right onto Heavy Equipment School Road. Parking is available near the dead end of this road. (See map on page 80.)

The scenic lakeside town of Tega Cay, sitting on a 1,600-acre peninsula on the south end of Lake Wylie, offers a public golf course and driving range for those inclined to stay off the water. A 1.8-mile walking trail starts at **Trailhead Park** and travels through the wooded and residential sections of town, as well as along the golf course. If you're in the mood for a picnic, try either **Windjammer Park** or **Pitcarin Park**, both of which are located in Tega Cay. Windjammer Park, on Windjammer Road, includes a picnic area with shelters and tables, a

(continued to page 81)

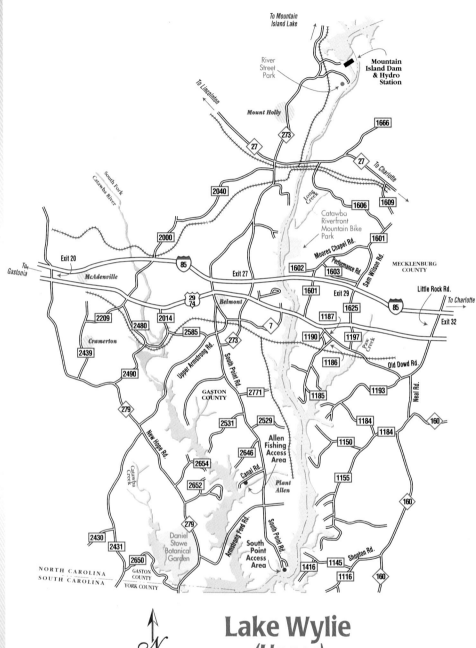

To Mountain Island Lake

River Street Park

Mountain Island Dam & Hydro Station

Mount Holly

To Lincolnton

1666

273

27

27

To Charlotte

South Fork Catawba River

2040

Long Creek

Catawba Riverfront Mountain Bike Park

1606

1609

2000

Moores Chapel Rd.

1601

Exit 20

1602

1603

Performance Rd.

MECKLENBURG COUNTY

To Gastonia

85

McAdenville

Exit 27

Sam Wilson Rd.

1601

Exit 29

Little Rock Rd.

To Charlotte

29 74

Belmont

1187

1625

85

Exit 32

2209

2480

2014

273

1190

1197

Paw Creek

2585

1186

Old Dowd Rd.

Cramerton

2439

Upper Armstrong Rd.

South Point Rd.

1185

1193

Neal Rd.

2490

2771

279

GASTON COUNTY

2531

2529

1184

160

New Hope Rd.

Allen Fishing Access Area

2646

1150

1184

Catawba Creek

2654

Canal Rd.

Plant Allen

1155

160

2652

279

Daniel Stowe Botanical Garden

Armstrong Ferry Rd.

South Point Rd.

South Point Access Area

1145

Shopton Rd.

2430

2431

1416

1116

160

2650

NORTH CAROLINA
SOUTH CAROLINA

GASTON COUNTY
YORK COUNTY

Lake Wylie
(Upper)

0   0.625"

1 mile

(continued from page 87)
swimming beach and a playground. Pitcarin Park has a lake access ramp, playground, basketball courts and a barbecue pit. (See map on page 82.)

A 26-acre park in York County, **Ebenezer Park**, offers a combination of recreation and relaxation. The park is a popular camping area since it has 71 wooded campsites overlooking the lake with electric, water and sewer hookups. Four picnic shelters, one large shelter and several open-air tables are available; each table has a grill. A swimming area at Ebenezer Park is open Memorial Day weekend through Labor Day and supervised by lifeguards. The park is located off Gallant Road in Rock Hill. (See map on page 82.)

One of the newer parks along the Catawba corridor is **River Park**, a 75-acre site in Rock Hill with a canoe launch and two miles of riverside trails. This park is a designated bird and wildlife preserve and offers hikers a chance to experience the wildlife habitats found along the free-flowing river. River Park is at 1782 Quality Circle in Rock Hill, SC. (See map on page 82.)

Perhaps more importantly, River Park also offers new access to the free-flowing section that begins south of Lake Wylie — a 30-mile segment that snakes its way through York, Chester and Lancaster counties. Along this route, we're reminded of the freedom this river once had and the power that attracted so much industry. At Landsford Canal, remnants of the channels and locks that once tried to tame the river are still visible. **Landsford Canal State Park** (See page 95 for details) offers recreation and history lessons on the banks of the Catawba River. Also

nearby is the **Catawba Cultural Center**, which offers a look into the history of the Catawba Indians.

The **Palmetto Paddling Company**, based in Rock Hill, SC, offers canoe and kayaking rentals and custom tours of the Catawba River. A popular tour begins at the Fort Mill Access Area below the dam on Lake Wylie and meanders along the free-flowing Catawba to River Park. Call (803) 482-3387 for information.

Lakeside Camping and Nearby Bed & Breakfasts

There are numerous camping facilities, hotels, motels and other lodging opportunities near the Catawba River. This list primarily includes riverside camping opportunities or Bed & Breakfasts. These inns provide a comfortable alternative to camping, and allow visitors to experience the sights and recreation of the river in a multi-day experience.

McDowell Nature Preserve and Copperhead Island Campgrounds: 39 camper and tent sites with electricity, grill and picnic table; 7 rent-a-tent sites with tent, cots, electricity, grill and picnic table; 10 primitive sites with fire rings. Copperhead Island has 6 rent-a-tent sites on Lake Wylie. Information: See page 85 for more details.

Ebenezer Park: 71 full-service campsites. Bathhouse with hot showers available. 26 acres with boat ramp, swimming, fishing and picnic facilities. Located on Lake Wylie. Information: (803) 366-6620.

Lazy Daze Campground: 215 sites with water and electricity. Swimming pool, mini-golf, play

(continued to page 83)

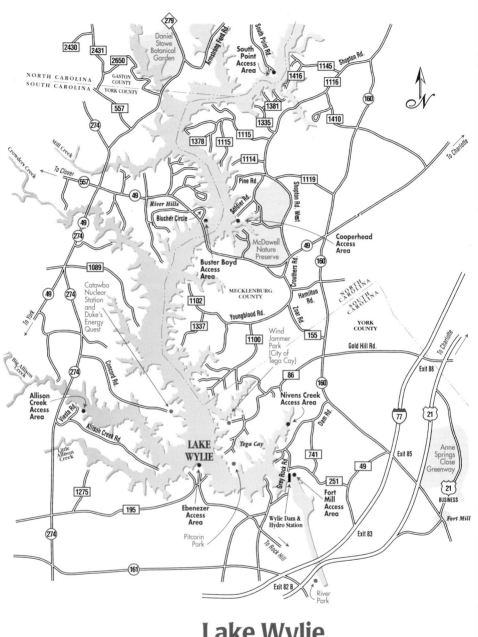

Lake Wylie
(Lower)

0   0.625"

1 mile

(continued from page 81)

ground, volleyball and game room. Store and laundry on-site. Information: 940 Gold Hill Road, Fort Mill, SC, (803) 548-1148.

Pine Lakes Campground: 108 sites with full hook-ups. Playground, picnic tables and grills. Stocked fishing pond. Information: 1802 SC 21, Fort Mill, SC, (803) 548-1111.

Homeleigh Bed and Breakfast: This Renaissance Revival home built in 1919 is listed on the National Register of Historic Places. Its 9,200 square feet offers five guest rooms, some with private terraces overlooking the gardens. Located in Belmont, NC, it is convenient to Daniel Stowe Botanical Gardens and Lake Wylie. Information: 411 N. Main Street, Belmont, NC, (704) 829-6264.

Still Waters Bed and Breakfast: This waterside retreat overlooks the Catawba River at the north end of Lake Wylie. Three guest rooms and a separate cottage with private baths are available, as well as a great room with a fireplace. Information: 6221 Amos Smith Road, Charlotte, NC, (704) 399-6299.

Harmony House Bed and Breakfast: This Victorian-style farmhouse offers a large veranda overlooking the pastoral views of this 36-acre retreat. Three guest rooms and one suite are furnished with antiques in addition to the common living room. Located in Rock Hill, south of Lake Wylie, this inn offers access to the free-flowing section of the Catawba River. Information: 3485 Harmony Road, Catawba, SC, (803) 329-5886 or (888) 737-0016.

Festivals and Events

Lake Wylie Splash Dash – June: The Lake Wylie Chamber of Commerce promotes several events every year including holiday gatherings, plant sales at Daniel Stowe Botanical Garden and this popular 10K, 5K and walk each June. Call (803) 831-2837 or visit the Chamber of Commerce web site for more information.

Celebrate America! Fourth of July Concert & Fireworks at Daniel Stowe Botanical Garden – July: There are events happening almost year-round at Daniel Stowe Botanical Garden, but this annual celebration is one of the best attended, with a spectacular firework display and music from the Charlotte Symphony. Call (704) 825-4490.

(continued to page 85)

Great egrets are often spotted along the Catawba River and especially in McDowell Nature Preserve during the spring and summer.

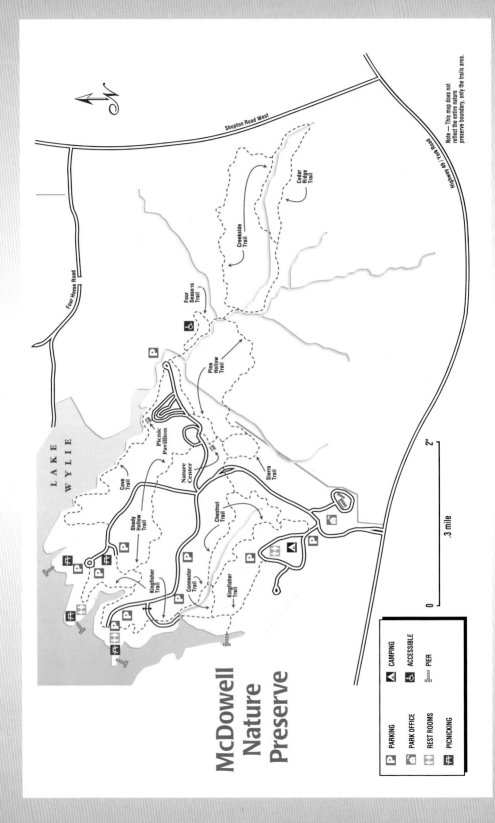

McDowell Nature Preserve

LAKE WYLIE

Shopton Road West

Four Horse Road

Highway 49 / York Road

Creekside Trail

Cedar Ridge Trail

Four Seasons Trail

Pine Hollow Trail

Picnic Pavillion

Nature Center

Cove Trail

Shady Hollow Trail

Sierra Trail

Chestnut Trail

Kingfisher Trail

Connector Trail

Kingfisher Trail

Note — This map does not reflect the entire nature preserve boundary, only the trails area.

0   .3 mile   2"

P PARKING	**▲** CAMPING
PARK OFFICE	**&** ACCESSIBLE
REST ROOMS	PIER
PICNICKING	

(continued from page 83)

Destinations: McDowell Nature Preserve

This 1,108-acre preserve on the shores of Lake Wylie was Mecklenburg County's first major park project in the mid-1970s. The fact that the preserve remains more than 90 percent undeveloped, however, is testament to its ecological significance. McDowell is home to a whopping 119 species of birds, 21 species of mammals, 21 species of reptiles and 14 species of amphibians. Scientists have documented many unusual finds here including the Loggerhead Shrike, Seminole bat and Gulf Coast spiny soft-shell turtle. Birding enthusiasts enjoy McDowell since they are all but assured of watching popular preserve denizens such as the Pileated woodpecker.

Ecological attractions aside, the park offers many recreational activities both within its boundaries and at nearby Copperhead Island. Powerboat ramp and canoe accesses as well as canoe and paddleboat rentals are available for water enthusiasts while some 6.6 miles of hiking trails and picnic areas give many opportunities for visitors to enjoy the scenic views and natural habitats found within the preserve. A campground with 56 sites accommodating tents and RVs is also located on-site. Visitors to the preserve can explore the Nature Center, which hosts numerous interactive displays.

McDowell opened in 1976 with a donation of 136 acres from Crescent Resources, then a subsidiary of Duke Power. The additional acreage was purchased in the following years, some of which was the site of a 1930 western-themed amusement park called Little Dodge City.

Location and hours: From Interstate 77 near the NC/SC border, take Exit 90 onto Carowinds Boulevard. Continue west three miles to NC 49. Turn left and travel four miles. The McDowell Nature Preserve entrance is on the right. (See maps on pages 82 and 84.)

The Nature Preserve is open daily from 7 a.m. to sunset. An entrance fee is charged March 1 through October 31 on weekends and holidays only. The fees are $3 per vehicle for county residents, $5 per vehicle for non-county residents and $2 for seniors. The Nature Center is open from 9 a.m. to 5 p.m. Monday through Saturday and holidays, 1 p.m. to 5 p.m. on Sundays. Admission is free. Additional charges apply for camping, boating and picnic shelter rentals.

Things to do: Definitely start at the Nature Center, which houses an impressive collection of exhibits to entertain and educate. The extensive live and interactive displays include "Living with Insects," "Life as an Insect" and "Insects in Nature" (notice a theme?). Add to that bats and frogs, birds and butterflies, and the nature center manages to intrigue its visitors both young and old. A classroom, gift counter and staff offices are also located here. Outside the nature center, bird-feeding stations and gardens provide a glimpse of nature for those who choose not to venture onto the trails. Find the Nature Center by entering the preserve and traveling past the campground and entrance booth. Turn right before the Y-intersection and proceed to the Nature Center parking lot.

Hiking is an exceptionally popular pastime at McDowell since the trails are often short, well-blazed loops. For a study in contrasts, hike the 0.5-mile long Cedar Ridge Trail (accessible only by the Creekside loop) for stellar views of the bottomland forest or select the 1.2-mile Chestnut Trail, which passes underneath a dense canopy of hickory and tulip poplar.

Copperhead Island, located on Lake Wylie just across from McDowell Nature Preserve, features 14 acres of waterfront with camp-sites, fishing piers, boat ramps, picnic areas and a paved trail around the island. For Copperhead Island, from Carowinds Boulevard and NC 49, take NC 49 south three miles to Shopton Road. Turn right and travel two miles to Pine Harbor Road. Turn left, then immediately left again onto Soldier Road. Follow to the end.

For more information: McDowell Nature Preserve, 15222 York Road, Charlotte, NC 28078, (704) 588-5224.

Destinations: Daniel Stowe Botanical Gardens

Daniel Stowe Botanical Gardens occupies 450 acres along the northern shores of Lake Wylie. Still in its early stages of development, there are currently 110 acres open to the public, offering an outstanding floral composition of colors, shapes, sizes, textures and, yes, scents. The gardens are the vision of Daniel Stowe, a former textile executive, who created the center and provided a $14 million endowment to ensure its future. Visitors can enjoy four extensive gardens featuring a dozen fountains, sculptures and wooden trellises. The Robert Lee Stowe Pavilion acts as the visitor center for the gardens and creates a gateway to the grounds. Additionally there is a woodland nature trail accessed from the visitor center, which winds through the forested areas of the park.

Location and hours: From Interstate 85 west of Charlotte, take Exit 20 in Gastonia. Follow NC 279 south for 10 miles. The entrance will be on the right. (See map on page 82.)

Daniel Stowe Botanical Gardens is open daily from 9 a.m. to 5 p.m. and closed Thanksgiving, Christmas and New Year's Day. Admission is $8 per person for adults, $4 per person for children 6 to 12 and free for children under 6 and members.

The Pavilion: The stylish architec-ture of this 13,500-square-foot building welcomes visitors as they enter the gardens from the main drive. Once inside, a large diorama shows the expansive layout of the grounds, including undeveloped areas. The center court of the pavilion is a large glass enclosed room, which allows the first of four gardens to beckon visitors through the patio doorways. The side wings of the building house educational classrooms, restrooms, an informa-tion stand and displays. A gift shop offers natural floral gifts, t-shirts, hats, jewelry and other floral- or bird-themed gift items. A large selection of books, as well as an outdoor patio with plants and pottery, is also on-site.

The Grounds: The gardens at Daniel Stowe offer year-round enjoy-ment. The Four Seasons Garden greets visitors as they exit the

Daniel Stowe Botanical Garden is a magnificent ode to flora even in its early stages of development.

pavilion, and mixes evergreens with perennials and annuals to ensure color for every season. The long trellised walkways flanking the center garden are covered in climbing vines. These lead visitors to the Cottage Garden and the first of many fountains found throughout the gardens. A more traditional garden, this display includes a variety of recognizable blooms such as hollyhock and roses.

Continue on to the Canal Garden where a center channel of water with unique fish sculptures adds to the sights and scents of the garden. The Perennial Garden offers long, circular walkways and patterns through many familiar and unfamiliar displays of color. Fountains and sculptures are elegantly placed throughout the gardens. At the far end of the garden tour, a new area under development hints at the expansions to come at Daniel Stowe. This Conifer Garden will feature evergreens in a showy mix of form and texture. At this point, a tramcar is available to escort visitors back to the Pavilion.

For more information: Call (704) 825-4490 or visit the garden's web site (see appendix).

Day Trips: Anne Springs Close Greenway

The Anne Springs Close Greenway in Fort Mill, SC is a visionary conservation achievement that mixes history with recreation amenities such as mountain bike trails. Opened in 1995, the 2,300-acre greenway is more of an active nature preserve than a traditional (linear) greenway. The land, which has been in the Close family for more than 200 years, was a gift to the citizens of Fort Mill by members of the Close family who sought to establish a buffer against urban encroachment from the

(continued to page 89)

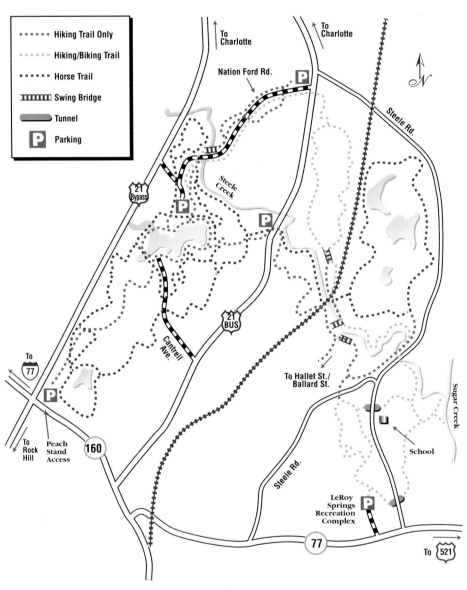

Anne Springs Close Greenway

(continued from page 87)
Charlotte area. Today, the greenway's hickory-dogwood forests and 30-acre Lake Haigler form a graceful arc around the city of Fort Mill, but this land has been special to the Catawba River region for thousands of years.

The greenway is home to two barns for events and informal gatherings, a nature center, a historic log cabin and a bat house. Additionally, greenway staff often perform recreation and interpretive programs such as "Ecology Institute" and "History in a Backpack" programs for local schoolchildren. For our purposes, though, the biggest attraction at the greenway is its 32-mile network of hiking, mountain biking and equestrian trails. Among the most popular trails are:

1. *Mountain Biking*: Springfield Loop (3.3 miles)
2. *Hiking and Handicapped Access*: Lake Haigler Trail (one mile) and Handicapped Trail (0.75 mile, concrete surface)
3. *Equestrian*: Blue Trail (5.1 miles) and Orange Trail (6.7 miles). The equestrian facilities at the greenway also include guided rides, private lessons and periodic overnight trips. Pre-registration is necessary for all trail rides.

It is best to check out a map at one of the entrances to the greenway since the trail network grows every year. Opening and closing times are posted at all trailheads; remember that no motorized equipment of any type is allowed on the trails. Hikers may use all trails but equestrians and mountain bikers must stay on designated trails.

Interestingly, some of the trails inside the greenway run atop or beside a historically significant trail called the Nation Ford Road. More than 300 years ago, trappers and settlers used this trail that – even prior to then – had been part of a Catawba Indian trading path extending from Florida to Pennsylvania. Eventually, the road became a part of the Great Philadelphia wagon road that stretched from Philadelphia to Savannah, Georgia, and was probably the first major road in the Eastern United States.

Directions: From Charlotte, travel south on Interstate 77 to Exit 85 for SC 160. Travel east toward Fort Mill crossing the US 21 bypass and continuing 0.7 mile to US 21 (business). Turn left and travel about 2.5 miles to the Dairy Barn entrance. Turn left onto the gravel road and follow to a parking lot and fee station on the left at 0.3 mile. (See map on pages 82 and 88.)

Open: Daily

Admission: Admission is free for members of the greenway or $2 per person for hiking and mountain biking, $5 for horseback riding and $8 for primitive camping with bathhouse privileges (reservations are required).

For more information: Visit the greenway online (see appendix) or call (800) 770-6967.

Anne Springs Close Greenway offers many opportunities for equestrians.

Osprey with fresh catch over the Catawba River.

Fishing Creek Lake, Great Falls & Stumpy Pond

The Catawba's free flow south of Lake Wylie passes through some isolated and wooded countryside until it begins a gradual widening into Fishing Creek Lake, a modest reservoir consisting of 3,112 acres of surface area and 61 miles of shoreline. This long narrow lake separates Chester and Lancaster counties in South Carolina and joins Fishing Creek, a popular day float among local paddlers. Below Fishing Creek Lake, a series of islands divides the Catawba in a jumbled maze of lakes, shoals and hydro stations. Little-explored except by adventuresome anglers and hunters, the Catawba here is home to an array of wildlife and remains one of the most fantastic areas on the entire corridor.

The first island in this chain is Mountain Island, a hulking mass of rock that gives the area an Appalachian flavor. It is not easy to reach and has no public facilities. South of this island, Dearborn Island (also known as Big Island) sits like a huge Rorschach blob smack in the middle of the Catawba. Pickett Island and several smaller islands pepper the water on the east side of Dearborn. Here, most locals also know the Catawba as Stumpy Pond (or Cedar Creek Reservoir if you want to be official). On the west side of Dearborn Island, the Catawba is known as Great Falls Reservoir — so named for the river's rocky drop near the current Great Falls Hydro Station — an 847-acre lake with some 20 miles of shoreline, most of it heavily wooded. Between the two lakes, there are four hydroelectric stations: Great Falls, Dearborn, Rocky Creek and Cedar Creek.

Location

The three lakes parallel US 21 in Chester County, SC and Interstate 77 slightly further west.

Recreation: Paddling, Biking and Fishing

While public access points provide ramps for motorboats, these lakes and their tributaries draw the attention of many canoeing and kayaking enthusiasts since their waters are calm and quiet. Many areas of shallow water and protected coves provide excellent havens for waterfowl and other wildlife viewing. Fishing is also popular and a great way to enjoy the serenity of these smaller lakes. The banks of **Fishing Creek Lake** are relatively free from development and are largely forested. It is popular for paddlers to put-in at the SC DNR Highway 9 Access Area west of Lancaster and paddle the entire lake in an easy trip.

Although we haven't spent much time discussing Catawba tributaries to this point, local paddlers say the adventurous float on **Fishing Creek** is one of South Carolina's finest creeks. Wildlife such as otters, beavers and turkey are abundant on this circuitous creek and there are plenty of places for backcountry camping, fishing and backwoods tomfoolery. Although it may require

(continued to page 93)

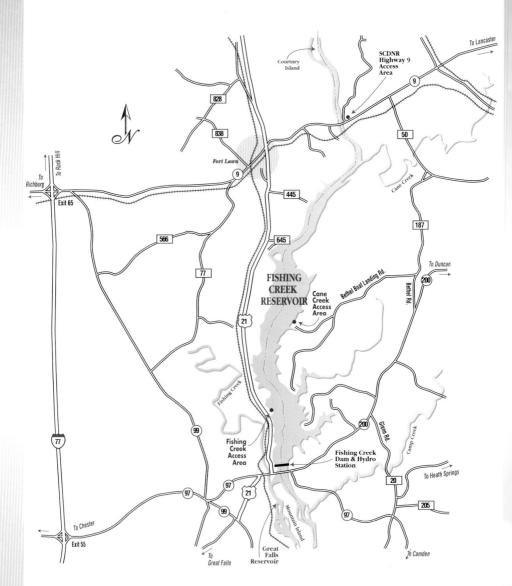

Fishing Creek Reservoir

(continued from page 91)

occasional portages around sand bars, the creek is best to float when it is at medium or low levels (or when the water is one-quarter to one-half the width of the creek). This trip takes about five hours if you put-in on Hightower Road in Great Falls and take-out at Fishing Creek Dam. To find the put-in from the only traffic light in Great Falls, SC, drive west on US 21 toward Chester for approximately one mile and make a right turn onto SC 99. Follow SC 99 to Hightower Road (Chester County Road 77) and turn right. Follow to a bridge and unmarked put-in.

Rivertown Outfitters — which offers canoe and kayak rentals, tours and instruction on the Catawba near Great Falls — services all of the paddling areas described in this section. Call (803) 482-3387 for information. Also, **Carolina Kayaks and Canoes** in Great Falls, SC offers portages, rentals and more. Call (803) 482-3387.

Lakeside Camping and Nearby Bed & Breakfasts

Although it is possible to camp in primitive locations along the river, there are no public riverside camping opportunities on this section of the Catawba. *Note:* Landsford Canal State Park does not allow camping.

Wade-Beckham House: This plantation house built in 1832 is listed on the National Register of Historic Places. Three guest rooms overlook 500 acres of rural farm property and old stone outbuildings. Information: 3385 Great Falls Hwy, Lancaster, SC, (803) 285-1105.

Kilburnie: The Inn at Craig Farm: Built in downtown Lancaster, SC in 1827 and moved to its current location on historic Craig Farm in 1999, this inn is believed to be the oldest surviving dwelling in the city. The inn has five rooms, each with fireplace and bath. Information: 1824 Craig Farm Road, Lancaster, SC 29720, (803) 416-8420.

Festivals and Events

Lily Fest — May: This celebrated event showcases the rare Rocky Shoals Spider lily as it blooms in masses within Landsford Canal State Park. With one of the largest known concentrations of this rare flower, Landsford Canal makes a spectacular setting for this annual hike. Music and other activities are also scheduled throughout the day. For information, contact (803) 789-5800.

Flopeye Fish Festival — May: This annual food festival held each Memorial Day weekend in Great Falls, SC is extremely popular. The festival includes a carnival, car show, music and plenty of local food. Call (803) 482-6029.

River Moon Festival — June: This festival located at the Catawba Cultural Center features storytelling and enactments of Catawba folklore and legends. Native American foods are available for sampling. Other events include gardening and archaeology lessons and exhibits. For information, contact (803) 328-2427.

(continued to page 95)

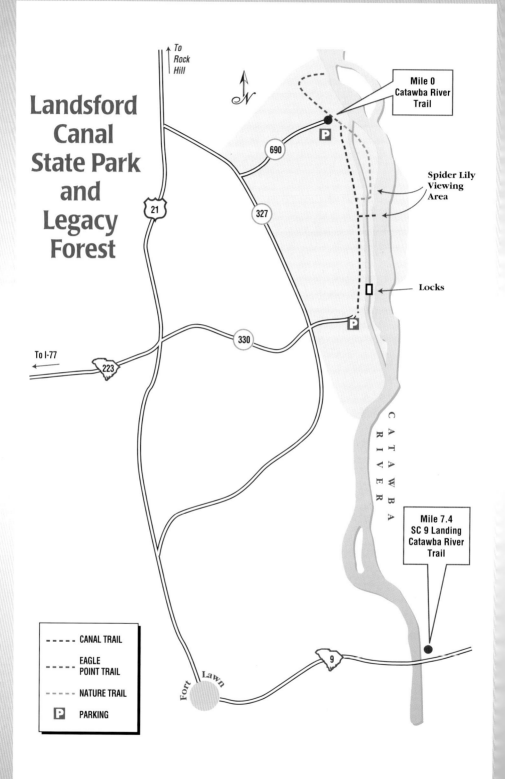

Landsford Canal State Park and Legacy Forest

To Rock Hill

N

21

690

327

330

223

To I-77

Mile 0 Catawba River Trail

P

Spider Lily Viewing Area

Locks

P

CATAWBA RIVER

Mile 7.4 SC 9 Landing Catawba River Trail

9

Fort Lawn

- - - - CANAL TRAIL

- - - - EAGLE POINT TRAIL

- - - - NATURE TRAIL

P PARKING

(continued from page 93)

Great Falls Heritage Celebration – October: This locally popular gathering celebrates the cultural and natural history of the Great Falls area and the Catawba River. Call (803) 482-2370.

Yap Ye Iswa – November: The "Day of the Catawbas" festival is held annually at the Catawba Indian Reservation on the Saturday after Thanksgiving. The festival focuses on Catawba Indian history and heritage. Handmade pottery is crafted and sold throughout the day. Traditional Catawba food such as fry bread, Indian tacos, venison and roasted corn are among the offerings. For information, contact (803) 324-0259.

Destinations: Landsford Canal State Park

Really just a blip on your highway map, Landsford, South Carolina is a lonely place for much of the year. A dilapidated grocery and directional sign mark a turn off US 21 for the park entrance. We're not far from the textile town of Lancaster, but we might as well be on our way to the moon… a definite plus for backcountry types!

Landsford Canal State Park was created in 1970 because it is home to a canal that is the best-preserved type of this structure in South Carolina. There is a remarkable amount of history here. A ford over the Catawba (Land's Ford) was probably named for settler Thomas Land

who received a land grant in 1755. The ford was used by both Patriot and British armies during the American Revolution, but was later deemed impassable by engineers looking for a trade-worthy waterway between mountains and sea. Soon afterward, the Landsford Canal was built as the uppermost of four canals on the Catawba between 1820 and 1835. It was intended for use by ferryboats hoping to bypass a stretch of rapids and rocky shallows. However, the canal only served its function for a few years in the 1820s then was completely abandoned by 1846, victim to railroads and a better highway system. But an engineering folly is our gain since the canal essentially preserved the "rocky shoals" habitat on the river itself. Some naturalists believe this habitat was more common before the Catawba was heavily impounded in the last century.

A great blue heron ready to take flight at Landsford Canal.

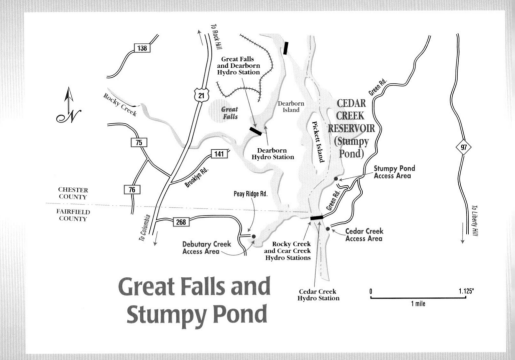

Great Falls and Stumpy Pond

Map labels:

138

To Rock Hill

Great Falls and Dearborn Hydro Station

Rocky Creek

21

Great Falls

Dearborn Island

Green Rd.

CEDAR CREEK RESERVOIR (Stumpy Pond)

75

141

Dearborn Hydro Station

Pickett Island

97

Brooklyn Rd.

Stumpy Pond Access Area

CHESTER COUNTY

76

Peay Ridge Rd.

Green Rd.

FAIRFIELD COUNTY

To Columbia

268

Debutary Creek Access Area

Rocky Creek and Cear Creek Hydro Stations

Cedar Creek Access Area

To Liberty Hill

Cedar Creek Hydro Station

0   1.125"

1 mile

Location and hours: From Charlotte, travel south on Interstate 77. Take Exit 77 onto US 21 south (traveling away from Rock Hill) and drive for 10 miles until US 21 becomes a two-lane road. Turn left onto Landsford Road and drive two miles. The park entrance is on the left. (See map on page 94.)

The park is open Thursday through Monday, 9 a.m. to 6 p.m., closed Tuesdays and Wednesdays. Call for details on the annual Lily Fest celebration each May. Admission is $1.50 per person for adults, free for children 15 and under and seniors 65 and older.

Things to do: If Landsford Canal is relaxing and quiet much of the year, it's certainly not between mid-May and mid-June. During this time the world's largest colony of the Rocky Shoals Spider lily blooms in a spectacular display that attracts floral enthusiasts from around the Southeast. Other natural wonders — fall foliage, Lowcountry sunrises — may get more attention, but Landsford Canal is one of a few places where you will hear grown men gasp at the sight of a gangly, snow-white flower (see page 30 for more about the Spider lily).

Hikers can also enjoy a stroll along the riverbanks or to the old canal on one of the park's two named trails, the Nature Trail and the Canal Trail. A mature riparian forest of tall oak, sweetgum, hickory and river birch surrounds the park, which is sandwiched by parking areas for convenient access. Birding enthusiasts can usually find something here year-round although the best seasons are spring and fall. The species to look for include bald eagles, prothonotary warblers (April through August), migrant warblers (April–May and September–October) and scarlet tanagers (mid-April through October).

In 2002, state-owned land at Landsford Canal nearly tripled in size when Crescent Resources agreed to sell 1,049 acres adjacent to the SC Department of Natural Resources as a Legacy Forest. The new property extends the boundary of the public land at Landsford west to Landsford Road, providing an additional riparian buffer, and extends the public-owned river frontage by almost a mile. It will allow for many additional recreational facilities in the future. This was the second expansion at Landsford in the last decade. In 1996, the Katawba Valley Land Trust assisted the SC Department of Parks, Recreation and Tourism in obtaining 210 acres of land on the east side of the Catawba River in Lancaster County for the park, nearly doubling the original 238-acre park.

For more information: Landsford Canal State Park, 2051 Park Drive, Catawba, SC 29704. Visit the park online (see appendix) or call (803) 789-5800.

Destinations: Catawba Cultural Center

The Catawba River valley has long been the home of the Catawba Nation and this rich heritage lives on at the Catawba Cultural Center. The center is located on the 640-acre Catawba Indian Reservation along the river near Rock Hill, South Carolina. Exhibits, displays and presentations educate visitors in

(continued to page 99)

Pottery has long been a major part of the Catawba Indian culture. Earl Robbins, above, is one of the nation's finest potters.

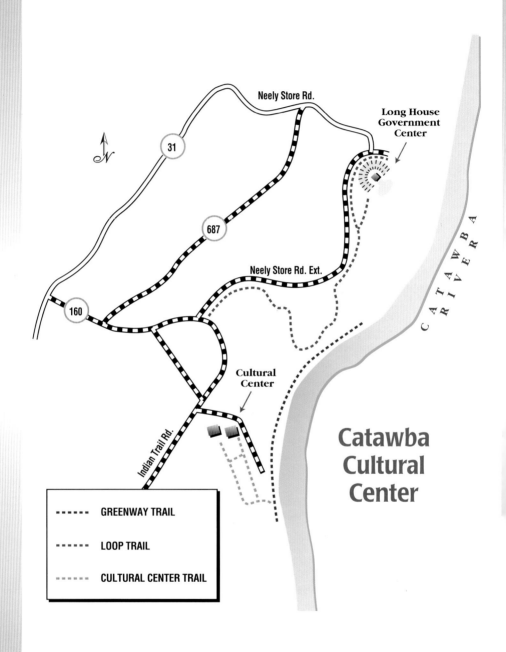

Neely Store Rd.

31

687

160

Neely Store Rd. Ext.

Long House
Government
Center

Cultural
Center

Indian Trail Rd.

C A T A W B A
R I V E R A

Catawba
Cultural
Center

- - - - - GREENWAY TRAIL

- - - - - LOOP TRAIL

- - - - - CULTURAL CENTER TRAIL

(continued from page 97)

Catawba culture and heritage. The center hosts storytelling and pottery-making events while the surrounding Catawba lands are home to numerous archaeological sites, agricultural displays, nature trails and a picnic area. Also located near the Catawba Cultural Center is the Long House, where tribal members hold government meetings.

Location and hours: The Catawba Cultural Center is located on the west side of the Catawba River at 1536 Tom Stevens Road, Rock Hill, SC. It is open Monday to Saturday from 9 a.m. to 5 p.m. The trails and grounds are open during daylight hours. Admission is free.

Things to do: There are three hiking trails awaiting visitors to the Cultural Center. The Loop Trail is 0.8 miles and starts at the Long House. This interpretive trail features a Catawba dwelling and dugout trees as well as an archaeological dig center. The Greenway Trail is 0.7 miles and starts at the Cultural Center along with the 0.5-mile Center Trail. The trails focus on the history of the area and the cultural aspects of Catawba Indian life. As you walk along the Catawba River, you are retracing a path used by some of the earliest inhabitants of South Carolina.

The tradition of Catawba Indian pottery that has survived for over 4,500 years still lives on at the Catawba Nation. Many of the residents here, including children, still make and sell pottery. Classes are taught and exhibitions are held in hopes of keeping this cultural tradition alive. Catawba potters still dig clay, hand-build and fire their craft despite the more modern techniques introduced over the centuries. North of the Catawba Nation, settlers of German descent have influenced much of the Catawba valley pottery still made; while the pottery made on the Reservation has remained pure to its original art form. The Catawba Cultural Center displays pottery for visitors to enjoy and hosts events which focus on teaching, exhibiting and selling Catawba Indian pottery.

The Catawba Cultural Preservation Project provides educational opportunities with its ongoing archaeological research program. Volunteer participation in seasonal fieldwork is encouraged and coordinated with the Archaeological Society of South Carolina. Numerous sites within the Reservation are studied for early evidence of life along the Catawba River valley. The program offers an opportunity to investigate and record these traces, and preserve the cultural heritage it supports.

For more information: Call (803) 328-2427 or visit the center online (see appendix).

Fishing is one of the biggest reasons to visit Lake Wateree.

Lake Wateree

With 13,864 acres of surface area and 242 miles of shoreline, Lake Wateree provides a wonderful end point for the Catawba and also serves as the beginning of the Wateree River. There are eight public access areas as well as numerous private marinas and access areas. Lake Wateree State Recreation Area lies on the western side of the lake in Fairfield County and ranks as one of the premier fishing destinations in the Midlands of South Carolina — if not the state. The lake acts as the border between Fairfield and Kershaw counties before lying entirely within Kershaw on the southern end.

Although there is not an abundance of land-based recreation on Lake Wateree other than the state recreation area, the lake does maintain a natural feel because of the largely rural surrounding communities. Pure and simple, though, this is bass country. If you pull into Lake Wateree State Recreation Area most anytime you can't miss the fact that fisherman of all makes and sizes love this lake!

Location

Lake Wateree parallels Interstate 77 as it runs south through Fairfield County, South Carolina. The eastern shores of the lake can be reached from SC 97 in Kershaw County, SC.

Recreation: Paddling, Biking and Fishing

As a large lake in the Piedmont region of South Carolina, Lake Wateree calls to water sport enthusiasts. Boating activities are popular, evident by the many public ramps, marinas and landings. Lake Wateree is a favorite among fishermen, known for its quiet coves and abundant fish population.

Lakeside Camping and Nearby Bed & Breakfasts

There are numerous camping facilities, hotels, motels and other lodging opportunities near the Catawba River. This list primarily includes riverside camping opportunities or Bed & Breakfasts. These inns provide a comfortable alternative to camping, and allow visitors to experience the sights and recreation of the river in a multi-day experience.

Lake Wateree State Recreation Area: 72 sites, water and electric, some on water's edge. Also features 2 bathhouses with hot showers and a camp *(continued to page 103)*

South Carolina naturalist Rudy Mancke keeps his students enraptured with tales of the Catawba.

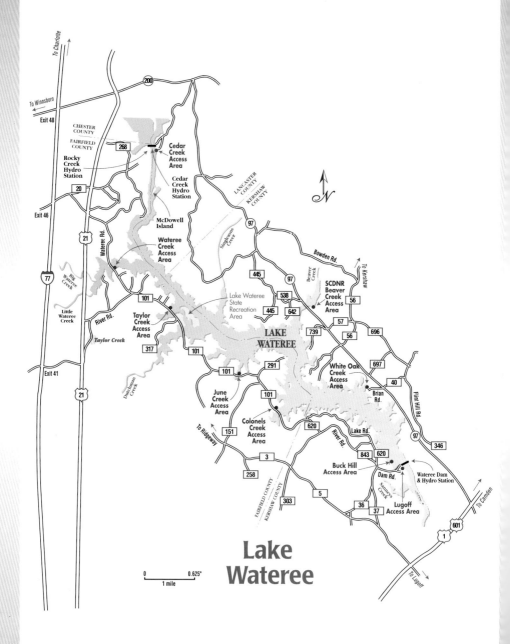

Lake
Wateree

To Charlotte

To Winnsboro

Exit 48

CHESTER COUNTY
FAIRFIELD COUNTY

268
Rocky Creek Hydro Station

Cedar Creek Access Area

Cedar Creek Hydro Station

20

Exit 46

McDowell Island

21

Wateree Rd.

Wateree Creek Access Area

77

Big Wateree Creek

Little Wateree Creek

LANCASTER COUNTY
KERSHAW COUNTY

97

Singleton Creek

101

River Rd.

Taylor Creek Access Area

Taylor Creek

317

Exit 41

101

21

Dutchman Creek

445

Bowden Rd.

Beaver Creek

To Kershaw

97

SCDNR Beaver Creek Access Area

56

Lake Wateree State Recreation Area

538

445

642

57

LAKE WATEREE

739

56

696

101

291

White Oak Creek Access Area

697

40

Brian Rd.

Flint Hill Rd.

101

June Creek Access Area

To Ridgeway

151

Colonels Creek Access Area

620

River Rd.

Lake Rd.

97

346

843

620

3

Buck Hill Access Area

Dam Rd.

Wateree Dam & Hydro Station

258

FAIRFIELD COUNTY
KERSHAW COUNTY

303

5

Sutton's Creek

36

37

Lugoff Access Area

601

1

To Camden

To Lugoff

0   0.625"
1 mile

(continued from page 101)
store on-site. Information: (see below) located on SC 101 east of I-77.

Wateree Lake Campground: 38 sites, 10 with full hook-ups and 28 with water and electricity. Bathhouse with hot showers, picnic area and camp store on-site. Information: 2367 Dolan Road, Liberty Hill, SC, (803) 273-3103.

Festivals and Events

Rock Around the Clock Festival – September: The Fairfield County Chamber of Commerce puts on this popular fall festival that includes an annual 5K run/walk, lots of classic cars and other amusements. (803) 635-4242.

Destinations: Lake Wateree State Recreation Area

This area consists of 238 acres on the western shore of Lake Wateree. A boat ramp and tackle shop anchor the area and provide support for lake recreation. An abundance of wildlife makes this a popular destination for other outdoor activities. Lake Wateree State Recreation Area offers nature trails, a picnic area and playground, and a large camping facility with 72 sites, some of which are located on the water's edge.

Location and hours: Lake Wateree State Recreation Area is located on SC 101 (Wateree Road), 11 miles east of Interstate 77. Lake Wateree State Recreation Area opens daily at 6 a.m. year-round. Evening hours are extended during Daylight Savings.

Park office hours are Monday to Friday from 9 a.m. to 5 p.m. (See maps on pages 102 and 104.)

Things to do: Similar to the Santee-Cooper lakes in South Carolina's Lowcountry, Lake Wateree has quite a reputation among local fishermen. In fact, many anglers consider it the most consistent bass and crappie lake in the entire region and one that also provides fine catfish and bream. Despite the ever-present power boats and numerous trailers, naturalists and wildlife-viewing aficionados should get plenty out of a trip to this park as well. To begin with, the Desportes Nature Trail offers an enjoyable 0.7-mile out-and-back hike along the lakeshore. Begin from either the parking area or from the trail entrance off the park road, then follow the level, easy trail out for a short loop onto a peninsula. Traffic is not heavy along this trail so there is a good chance that you may see wild turkey or deer along the lake and great blue herons or woodpeckers overhead.

(continued to page 105)

A pine warbler on the banks of the Catawba.

Lake Wateree
State Recreation Area

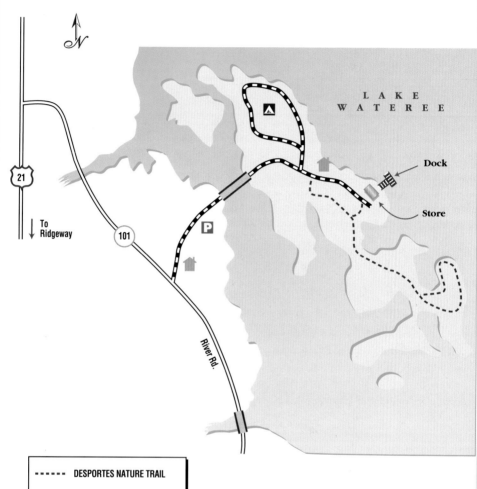

LAKE
WATEREE

Dock

Store

21

To
Ridgeway

101

River Rd.

- - - - - DESPORTES NATURE TRAIL

P PARKING

▲ CAMPING

🏠 PRIVATE RESIDENCE

(continued from page 103)

Since it is situated on a beautiful bluff above the lake and easily accessed by a loop road, camping at Lake Wateree State Natural Area is quite popular among both recreational campers and the fishing set. One note: The campground is fairly quiet and serene unless anglers' tournaments are held on the lake.

Although the park is extremely popular during the summer, Lake Wateree is an excellent destination for adventurous paddlers in search of solitude during the winter months. Since it is mostly natural, the lake offers prime opportunities for photography and it is easy to island hop or even stop off for picnics at nearby river access areas such as Taylor Creek.

For more information: Lake Wateree State Recreation Area, 881 State Park Road, Winnsboro, SC 29180. Visit the park online (see appendix) or call (803) 482-6401.

Day Trips: Fishing on the Catawba River

Deep bodies of water, narrow channels, shallow inlets, fast flowing rapids, standing pools – the Catawba River corridor offers many fish habitats. And for fishing enthusiasts, this chain of lakes and river is a home away from home. Some of the fish you may expect to catch along the waters of the Catawba include: largemouth bass, smallmouth bass, white bass, rainbow and brown trout, bluegill, black crappie, carp, striped bass and catfish.

But that list does not do justice to the array of species found between Lake James and Lake Wateree. Some of North Carolina and South Carolina's state fishing records have come from the waters of the Catawba. Luckily, the river is not just for the seasoned sport fisherman. The Catawba calls to everyone who just wants to drop a line, close their eyes against a mid-day sun and revel in the relaxation of the river.

Some of the most productive angling locations on the Catawba include the "tailwater" areas downstream of the hydro stations. Bank fishing access areas below the Wylie and Wateree hydro plants produce great catches for anglers year-round. And the trout fishery below the Bridgewater hydro station provides one of the river's most unique fishing opportunities.

Lake Norman, meanwhile, is one of the most popular fishing destinations in the region. Local bass tournaments seemingly take place daily while channel cat fishing is popular in the summer and stripers provide excellent action for live bait fishermen all year long. If your technique is good and you know where to go, the Catawba River and its lakes could keep you busy 24–7!

Public Lake Accesses

Refer to marked access points to the lake of your choice.

Additional Designated Fishing Areas

Bridgewater Fishing Area: This area is located below the dam at Lake James and is provided by Duke Power. (See map on page 36.)

Gentain are colorful wildflowers found along the Catawba River.

Huffman Bridge Access Area: This bank fishing area is located on Lake Rhodhiss along Huffman Bridge Road. (See map on page 44.)

River Bend Park: This 450-acre park is located below the dam at Lake Hickory. There is a bank fishing location along the river in the park. (See map on page 48.)

John Geitner Park: This city park and picnic area offers a fishing dock on Lake Hickory. (See map on page 46.)

Marshall Fishing Area: Duke built this designated fishing area on the banks of Lake Norman off NC 150. (See map on page 58.)

McGuire Fishing Area: A second designated fishing area on Lake Norman is located within the McGuire Station and Energy Explorium complex. (See map on page 58.)

Ramsey Creek Park: This county park and picnic area on Lake Norman has a fishing pier available for visitors. (See map on page 58.)

Latta Plantation Nature Preserve: This large preserve offers fishing opportunities within its 1,290 acres on Mountain Island Lake. (See map on page 68.)

Mountain Island Tailrace Fishing Area: Duke Power provides this fishing platform for bank fishing below the Mountain Island Dam and Hydro Station. (See map on 66.)

Allen Fishing Access Area: This bank fishing area is located on upper Lake Wylie off Canal Road. (See map on page 80.)

McDowell Nature Preserve: This expansive preserve offers numerous fishing areas and accesses on the shores of Lake Wylie. (See map on page 84.)

Fort Mill Access Area: Provides excellent bank fishing below the Wylie dam. (See map on page 80.)

Lugoff Access: Provides excellent year-round bank fishing below the Wateree hydro station. (See map on page 102.)

Charters and Guide Services

Chartered trips along the Catawba River and its lakes generally run from around $100 for a half day to more than $300 for a full day. The services listed below are only a small selection of the services offered along the Catawba.

Captain Darryl's Guide Service: This service offers trips on Lake Wylie, Rocky Creek Lake and Lake Wateree. The many locations offered by Captain Darryl include the rivers and tributaries that feed these lakes. Call (803) 324-7912.

Catawba Lakes Guide Service: With many years of fishing experience, this service offers charters on lakes James, Rhodhiss, Hickory and Norman. Located in Nebo, NC. Call (828) 205-1429.

Charlie's Charter Fishing: Located at the Lake James Landing, this charter service offers fishing trips on Lake James. All tackle provided. Call (828)-652-2907.

Lake Norman Ventures: With more than 40 years' experience on Lake Norman, this operation out of Mooresville is an excellent bet if you're intent on striper fishing. Call (704) 896-1704.

Quicksilver Guide Service: This 7-year-old guide service runs out of Mooresville, NC and takes striper and catfish trips on Lake Norman and Mountain Island Lake year-round. Call (704) 664-4523.

Silverhook Fishing: This service out of Mooresville, NC will take you looking for stripers, catfish and crappie on lakes Norman and Wylie. Instruction and guiding are both available. Call (704) 664-2220.

Bait and Tackle

There are far too many marinas and bait shops located along the lakes and river to mention on this page. The appendix section of this book includes marinas to contact for local fishing information.

Noteworthy

Fish are being used to improve the quality of our waterways and to control the impact of environmental hazards. For example, Hydrilla, an aquatic weed that grows uncontrollably when introduced in the lakes' waters, is a favorite food source of the grass carp. Therefore, thousands of sterile grass carp may be released and managed in lakes where Hydrilla becomes a problem for operators of water intakes or endangers public safety.

Another beautiful sunset on the Catawba.

Appendix

1. Freeze, Gary. *The Catawbans: Crafters of a North Carolina County, 1747–1900*. Catawba: The Catawba County Historical Association, 1995, p. 1.

2. Savage, Henry Jr. *River of the Carolinas: The Santee*. Chapel Hill, NC: University of North Carolina Press, 1968, p. 17.

3. Freeze 15.

4. Merrell, James H. *The Catawbas*. NY: Chelsea House Publishers, 1989, p. 36.

5. Personal library of Rock Hill historian Louise Pettus.

6. Freeze 15.

7. Kennedy, Billy. *The Scots-Irish in the Carolinas*. Northern Ireland: Causeway Press, 1997, p. 19.

8. Trimble, S.W. *Man-Induced Soil Erosion in the Southern Piedmont, 1700–1970*. Soil Conservation Society of America, 1974, p. 162.

9. Savage, 400.

10. Eller, William. *Mount Dearborn Military Establishment*. Abbeville, SC: Wiles Printing, 1999, p. 19.

11. Freeze 3.

12. Maynor, Joe. *Duke Power: The First 75 Years*. Self-published, 1980, p. 13.

13. Durden, Robert F. *Electrifying the Piedmont Carolinas*. Durham, NC: Carolina Academic Press, 2001, p. 34.

14. Durden 35.

15. Trimble 162.

16. Savage 400.

17. Savage 400.

18. Savage 401.

19. Durden 127.

Additional Resources

Able, Gene. *Exploring South Carolina: Wild and Natural Places*. Rock Hill, SC: Palmetto Byways Press, 1995.

Able, Gene and Jack Horan. *Paddling South Carolina*. Orangeburg, SC: Sandlapper Publishing Co., Inc., 2001.

Alden, Peter and Gil Nelson. *National Audubon Society Field Guide to the Southeastern States*. NY: Alfred A. Knopf, 1999.

Coggeshall, John M. *Carolina Piedmont Country*. Jackson, MS: University of Mississippi Press, 1996.

Cook, Dave. *The Piedmont Almanac: A Guide to the Natural World*. Chapel Hill, NC: Mystic Crow Publishing, 2001.

De Hart, Allen. *Hiking South Carolina Trails*. Old Sayebrook, CT: The Globe Pequot Press, 1998. Fourth edition.

Durden, Robert F. *Electrifying the Piedmont Carolinas*. Durham, NC: Carolina Academic Press, 2001.

Freeze, Gary. *The Catawbans: Crafters of a North Carolina County, 1747–1900*. Catawba: The Catawba County Historical Association, 1995.

Gaillard, Frye and Dot Jackson. *The Catawba River*. Boiling Springs: Gardner-Webb College Press, 1983.

Giffen, Morrison. *South Carolina: A Guide to Backcountry Travel &*

Adventure. Asheville, NC: Out There Press, 1997.

Hammond, Mary Ellen and Jim Parham. *Natural Adventures in the Mountains of Western North Carolina*. Almond, NC: Milestone Press, 1999.

Jacobs, Jimmy. *Trout Streams of Southern Appalachia*. Woodstock, VT: Backcountry Guides, 2001. Second edition.

Kennedy, Billy. *The Scots-Irish in the Carolinas*. Northern Ireland: Causeway Press, 1997.

Maynor, Joe. *Duke Power: The First 75 Years*. Self-published, 1980.

Merrell, James H. *The Catawbas*. NY: Chelsea House Publishers, 1989.

Savage, Henry Jr. *River of the Carolinas: The Santee*. Chapel Hill, NC: University of North Carolina Press, 1968.

Wyche, Thomas. *Mosaic: 21 Special Places in the Carolinas – The Land Conservation Legacy of Duke Power*. Englewood, CO: Westcliffe Publishers, 2002.

Brochures, Rare Publications & Pocket Guides

Wildflowers of the Catawba River Valley. Duke Power. Available at Duke Power's two visitor centers.

Catawba River Greenway: Tree Identification Guide. Available at Catawba River Greenway.

Checklist of the Birds of Mecklenburg County, NC Mecklenburg County Park and Recreation Department.

Eller, William. *Mount Dearborn Military Establishment*. Abbeville, SC: Wiles Printing, 1999.

Favorite Mountain Bike Trails of South Carolina. Columbia, SC: Palmetto Conservation Foundation, 1997.

Favorite Canoe & Kayak Trails of South Carolina. Columbia, SC: Palmetto Conservation Foundation, 1997.

Favorite Birding Trails of South Carolina. Columbia, SC: Palmetto Conservation Foundation, 1997.

Favorite Horse Trails of South Carolina. Columbia, SC: Palmetto Conservation Foundation, 1997.

Hickory, North Carolina: Metro Visitor Guide. Fall/Winter 2000.

The Catawba River Corridor Plan. SC Catawba River Task Force. SC DNR, SC PRT, Catawba Regional Council of Governments. 1994. 89 pp.

The Landsford West Expansion Tract. Landsford West Resource Team. Katawba Valley Land Trust. 2000.

Trimble, S.W. *Man-Induced Soil Erosion in the Southern Piedmont, 1700–1970*. Soil Conservation Society of America, 1974. 180 pp.

Web Sites

Anne Springs Close Greenway: www.leroysprings.com

Carolina Raptor Center: www.birdsofprey.org.

Catawba County Historical Association: www.catawbahistory.org

Catawba County: www.co.catawba.nc.us

Catawba Cultural Center: www.ccppcrafts.com

Catawba Lands Conservancy: www.catawbalands.org

Catawba Riverkeeper: www.catawbariverkeeper.org

Catawba Science Center: www.catawbascience.org

Catawba Valley Heritage Alliance: www.heritagealliance.org

Catawba Valley Scottish Society: www.lochnorman.org

Central Carolina Amphibian & Reptile Initiative: www.bio.davidson.edu/people/midorcas/CCARI/ccari.htm

City of Hickory Recreation Pages: www.ci.hickory.nc.us/recreation/

Daniel Stowe Botanical Garden: www.stowegarden.org

Duke Power: www.dukepower.com

Hickory Museum of Art: www.hickorymuseumofart.org

Historic Latta Plantation: www.lattaplantation.org

Katawba Valley Land Trust: www.kvlt.org

Lake Norman Convention and Visitors Bureau: www.lakenorman.org

Lake Norman Online Community: www.golakenorman.com

Lake Wylie Chamber of Commerce: www.lakewyliesc.com

Leave No Trace: www.lrt.org

McDowell County, NC: www.mcdowellnc.org

Mecklenburg Audubon Society: www.meckbirds.org

Mecklenburg County Parks & Recreation: www.parkandrec.com

National Park Service: www.nps.gov

North Carolina Division of Forest Resources: www.dfr.state.nc.us

North Carolina Division of Marine Fisheries: www.ncdmf.net

North Carolina Division of Parks and Recreation: www.ils.unc.edu/parkproject/ncparks.html

North Carolina Division of Tourism, Film and Sports Development: www.visitnc.com

North Carolina Wildlife Resources Commission: www.state.nc.us/wildlife

Paddling.net: www.paddling.net

Queens Landing: www.queenslanding.com

Rock Hill/York County Tourism & Sports Commission: www.yccvb.org

South Carolina Department of Natural Resources: www.dnr.state.sc.us

South Carolina Department of Parks, Recreation and Tourism: www.discoversouthcarolina.com

Tarheel Trailblazers: www.tarheel-trailblazers.com

York County Culture and Heritage Commission: www.yorkcounty.org

Boat Rentals, Parasailing and Fishing Guides

Captain Darryl's Guide Service: www.captaindarryl.com

Lake Norman Parasailing: www.lakenormanparasailing.com

Lake Norman Striper Swipers: www.lnssfishn.com

Lake Norman Ventures: www.lakenormanstriperfishing.com

Lake Norman Yacht Charters: www.lakenormancharters.com

Silverhook Fishing: www.geocities.com/silver-hook2000

Skipper's Dry Storage & Boat Rentals (Lake Norman): www.skippersdrystorage.com

Palmetto Conservation Foundation

The Palmetto Conservation Foundation is a non-profit organization based in South Carolina that seeks to conserve natural and cultural resources, preserve historic buildings and landmarks, and promote outdoor recreation through trails and greenways.

PCF Press is the publishing imprint of the Palmetto Conservation Foundation. Our publications promote access and appreciation for the region's natural and historic wonders.

To submit manuscripts or for inquiries about PCF Press:
PCF Press, Att: Editor
PO Box 1984, Spartanburg, SC 29304
For more information, visit
www.palmettoconservation.org

A list of our recent publications:

TURTLE TRACKS
Follows one family's annual visit to a Southeastern beach where a young girl learns first hand about loggerhead sea turtles. 32 pages, full color. Trade hardcover $12.95. ISBN 0-9679016-6-9.

THE WATERFALLS OF SOUTH CAROLINA (Second Edition)
This unique guide is an essential exploring companion for every resident or visitor to South Carolina's spectacular mountains. 80 pages, full color photographs and maps. Trade paperback $12.95. ISBN 0-9679016-5-0

THE PALMETTO TRAIL: LOWCOUNTRY GUIDE
Part travel planner, part hiking companion, the Lowcountry Guide features anecdotal tales plus a thorough description of the Palmetto Trail's 100+ route in this part of the state. 90 pages, 51 B&W photos, 5 color maps. Wire Binding $12.95. ISBN 0-9679016-2-6.

About The Photographer

Bill Price has been exploring the Catawba River region for decades. In the last three years, he spent parts of 250 days on the water to capture the images in The Catawba River Companion. At Catawba Falls, he slipped and broke his arm during a steep climb but still managed to shoot two rolls of film. Landsford Canal State Park manager Al James told The Charlotte Observer that Price is different from other nature photographers: "He's not a biologist, but he really studies habitats and individual species before he goes into the woods." Price, 45, lives in Cassatt, SC, which is about 75 miles southeast of Rock Hill, SC. He works at DuPont's Camden plant and photographs or paddles on his days off. Price only dropped one lens into the Catawba while shooting this book.

Visit his website at www.billpricephotography.com